MW00366138

TRANSLATION OF FILM/VIDEO TERMS INTO GERMAN

DIE UBERSETZUNG VON FILM/VIDEO FACHAUSDRÜCKEN INS DEUTSCHE

Compiled by:
Zussamenstellt:

VERNE CARLSON

TRANSLATION OF FILM/VIDEO TERMS INTO GERMAN

This is the second book of a series in the following languages:

Dies ist das zweite Buch einer Serie in den folgenden Sprachen:

Book 1 - French ISBN: 0-943288-00-2
Buch 1 - Französisch

Book 2 - German ISBN: 0-943288-01-0
Buch 2 - Deutsche

Book 3 - Italian ISBN: 0-943288-02-9
Buch 3 - Italien

Book 4 - Spanish ISBN: 0-943288-03-7
Buch 4 - Spanisch

Book 5 - Japanese ISBN: 0-943288-04-5
Buch 5 - Japanisch

Set of 5 ISBN: 0-943288-05-3

ISBN: 0-943288-01-0

1 2 3 4 5 6 7 8 9 10

Printed in the United States of America

A DOUBLE C Cc PUBLICATION

Cc

CONTENTS

INHALTSVERZEICHNIS

ACKNOWLEDGEMENT

With more and more Producers dispatching crews to every corner of this small planet the need for a book such as this is evident. It concentrates on certain words and phrases common to the film and television industries throughout the German-speaking world. When applied they can turn a crew stymied by a difference in language into a cohesive working group.

This book emerged from personal notes. Years ago, when working with a German film crew whose language is translated here, I began writing words and phrases heard most often in a workday so that I could better understand and be understood. It didn't take long to discover that, through consulting a cross-reference it was possible to easily and effectively communicate regardless of the language spoken. And get the work done.

Because my notes were incomplete I called on many friends for help. They readily responded when they understood what the project would accomplish.

Those who contributed their time and expertise to this series may not all speak the same language; what they do have in common, however, is a high regard for their chosen profession and the people who work in it.

The contributors to this book and what they do, follows:

Jürgen L. Karg has been a "film fan" since his early childhood. Although he became a sociologist he put as much energy into organizing the University film club as into

VORBEMERKUNG

Nachdem mehr und mehr Produzenten ihre Teams in alle Ecken dieser immer kleiner werdenen Welt senden, liegt es auf der Hand, dass ein Buch wie dieses gebraucht wird. Der Inhalt konzentriert sich auf bestimmte, häufig gebrauchte Wörter und Redewendungen in der deutschprachigen Film- und Fernsehindustrie. Ein Team hat durch dieses Handbuch die Möglichkeit, Verständigungsschwierigkeiten aus dem Weg zu gehen und als homogene Gruppe zu arbeiten.

Dieses Buch entstand aufgrund persönlicher Notizen. Als ich vor vielen Jahren mit einem deutschen Kamerateam arbeitete, fing ich an, mir die meistgebrauchten Wörter und Redewendungen aufzuschreiben, um mich damit besser verständigen zu können und um besser verstanden zu werden. Mein persönliches "Wörterbuch" wurde für mich am Drehort unentbehrlich.

Weil meine Notizen aber unvollkommen waren, bat ich einige meiner Freunde, mir bei der Vervollständigung zu helfen. Sie taten es gerne.

Die Personnen, die ihre Zeit und ihr Können für diese Serie von Wörterbüchern zur Verfügung stellten, sprechen zwar nich alle die gleiche Sprache, aber sie alle haben das gleiche Engagement für ihren Beruf und für die Leute die darin arbeiten.

Die Mitarbeiter dieses Buches stellen sich vor:

Jürgen L. Karg war schon in seiner frühen Kindheit ein "Filmfan". Auf der Universität verwendete er ebensoviel Energie für die Arbeit in einem Filmclub wie für seine

his other studies.

Jürgen has been an Executive Producer and Co-Director in production all over Europe for several years now, whereby he prefers to work on films which deal with themes of social relevance. As of today he has his own production company in Frankfurt.

Dr. Ingrid Aall is an Art Historian, Professor at California State University Long Beach. She has traveled and studied worldwide. Her expertise in more than five languages qualified her as an invaluable consultant on this series.

To them, my deepest appreciation.

VERNE CARLSON

Studien.

Jürgen arbeitet seit eineger Jahren als Produktionsleiter, Regieassistant und Co-Regisseur in verschiedenen Ländern Europas wobei er die Arbeit an Filmen mit sozial relevanten Themen bevorzugt. Seit diesem Jahr hat er eine eigene Produktionsfirma in Frankfurt an Main.

Dr. Ingrid Aall ist Kunsthistoriker, Professor and der Kalifornischen Staatlichen Universität in Long Beach. Ihre Reisen und Studien sind erdumfassend. Ihr Wissen in mehr als fünf Sprachen qualifiziert sie als unersetzbaren Berater fur diese Bucherreihe.

Ihnen allen mein herzlicher Dank.

VERNE CARLSON

HOW TO USE THIS BOOK

This first edition contains 16 chapters. Each chapter is titled by a general category that relates to a specific area of production.

Each category is divided into two pages. The number at the left of each page indicates the beginning of a new word or phrase on that page. Example:

ENGLISH	GERMAN
1. good	1. Gut
2. page	2. Seite
3. How do you say this word?	3. Wie sagen Sie dieses Wort?
4. What is this?	4. Was ist das?

By finding a word or phrase in your own language it is simple enough to run a finger across the page to the corresponding word or phrase and then speak, or indicate, the information you are trying to convey.

Good luck! Viel Glück!

Note: As with any work some terms will be left out, change with use, or be revised by adaptation to a new technology. Any reader so desiring to contribute corrections is most welcome to do so. However, individual contributions cannot be acknowledged due to the exigencies of production.

GEBRAUCHSANLEITUNG

Diese erste Ausgabe besteht aus 16 Kapiteln. Jedes Kapitel ist mit einem allgemeinen Begriff überschreiben, der ein spezifisches Arbeitsgebiet umfasst.

Jede Kategorie ist in zwei Seiten Aufgeteilt. Die Nummer links einer Seite zeigt den Beginn eines neuen Wortes oder einer neuen Redewendung an:

1. good	1. Gut
2. page	2. Seite
3. How do you say this word?	3. Wie sagen Sie dieses Wort?
4. What is this?	4. Was ist das?

Um ein Wort oder eine Redewendung in ihrer eigenen Sprache zu finden ist es genug mit dem Finger das entschprechende Wort oder die Redewendung auf der entsprechenden Seite zu finden und dann zu sagen oder auf die Information hinzuweisen was sie zu sagen versuchen.

Good luck! Viel Glück!

Anmerkung: Wie bei jeder anderen Arbeit werden einige Bezeichnungen ausgelassen sein, im Gebrauch verändert oder revidiert bei der Anpassung an neue Technologie. Auf der anderen Seite können wegen Produktions Erforderungen individuelle Beiträge nicht gewürdigt werden.

PRONUNCIATION

VOWELS, DIPHTHONGS, UMLAUTS

a,aa	(ah)	as in *pa*
ä	(ay)	long, as in *day*
ä	(eh)	short, as in *met*
ai	(eye)	as in *aisle*
au	(ow)	as in *howl*
e,ee	(ay)	long, as in *ray*
e	(eh)	short, as in *bed*
ei, ey	(eye)	as the *i* in *mine*
eu	(oy)	as in *boy*
i	(ih)	as in *sit*
ie,ih	(ee)	as in *piece*
ig	(ig)	as in *big* if in middle of a word
ig	(ick)	as in *pick* often at end of a word
o,oo,oh	(oh)	as in *hole*
ö	(uh)	as in *puff*
u,uh	(oo)	long, as in *lute*
u	(ew)	short, as in *put*
ü	(ew)	as the *ew* in *few*

CONSONANTS

f, k, l, m, n, p, & t are pronounced the same as in English.

b	(bee)	as in *beat*
b	(pee)	as the *p* in *beep* often at end of a word/syllable & before *st* or *t*
c	(ts)	as the *ts* in *its* before *ä, e, i, & y*

c	(k)	as in *cake*
ch	(kh)	soft, as the *ch* in *loch*
ch	(sh)	if in a word of foreign origin
chs	(x)	as the *x* in *fix*
d	(dee)	as in *dog*
dt	(tee)	as the *t* in *dolt* often at the end of a word
g	(guh)	as in *gobo*
g	(k)	as the *k* in *take* often at the end of a word
gn	(gn)	both the *g* and *n* are sounded as in *eggnog*
h	(h)	as in *hot*
h	(-)	silent if in the middle of a word
j	(yot)	as the *y* in *yes*
j	(zh)	as in *azure* if a word of foreign origin
kn	(kn)	both the *k* and *n* are sounded as in *acknowledge*
pf	(pf)	both the *p* and *f* are sounded as in *cupful*
ph	(f)	as in *photo*
s	(z)	as the *z* in *zip* at the beginning of a word
s,ss	(s)	as in *see* at end of a word or syl-lable
sch	(sh)	as the *sh* in *ship*

sp	(shp)	as *shp* if at the beginning of a word
sp	(sp)	as the *sp* in *spa* in the middle or end of a word
st	(sht)	as *sht* if at the beginning of a word
st	(st)	as the *st* in *stop* in the middle or end of a word
th	(t)	as the *t* in *tot*, *h* not pronounced
tion	(ts'yohn)	as *ts-yohn*
tz	(ts)	as the *ts* in *pets*
v	(eff)	as the *f* in *flag*
w	(vee)	as the *v* in *volt*
x	(ks)	as the *ks* in *packs*
y	(ew)	as the *ew* in *new*
z	(ts)	as the *ts* in *its*

NOTES

Animal Handlers:

01. Animal Trainer:

a. dog

b. horse

c. wild

d. domestic

02. Wrangler (livestock)

03. Wrangler (horses)

Art Department:

04. Art Director

05. Assistant Art Director

06. Set Decorator

07. Scenic Artist

08. Draftsman

PERSONAL

PEHR-ZOH-NAHL

Tierpfleger:

Teer-p'fleh-ger:

01. Tiertrainer:
    Teer-tray-ner:

    a. Hund
       Hoont

    b. Pferd
       P'fehrdt

    c. Wild
       Villt

    d. gezähmt
       geh-tsemt

02. Cowboy (Viehpfleger)
    Kow-boy (Fee-p'flehger)

03. Cowboy (Pferdfleger)
    Kow-boy (P'fehrt-fleh-ger)

Abteilung Für Künstlerische Gestaltung:

Ahp-tye-loong fewr Kewnst-lehr-ish Geh-shtahlt-oong;

04. Film-Architekt
    Film-Ar-khih-tekt

05. Assistent des Filmarchitekten
    Ah-sis-tent dehs Film-Ar-khih-tek-ten

06. Ausstatter
    Ows-shtaht-ter

07. Kunstmaler/Prospektmaler
    Koonst-mah-ler/Proh-spekt-mah-ler

08. Technischer Zeichner
    Tek-nish-er Tsy-khner

Camera:

09. Director of Photography

10. Camera Operator

11. 1st Assistant Photographer

12. 2nd Assistant Photographer

13. Film Loader

14. Cinematographer:

a. aerial

b. animation

c. documentary

d. newsreel

e. process (rear or front)

f. second unit

:. special effects

h. stop motion

Kamera:
Kah-may-rah:

09. Chefkameramann
Shef-kah-may-rah-mahn

10. Kameramann
Kah-may-rah-mahn

11. Erster Kameraassistent
Ayr-ster Kah-may-rah-ah-sis-tent

12. Zweiter Kameraassistent
Tsvy-ter Kah-may-rah-ah-sis-tent

13. Kameraassistent, für das Filmeinlegen
K.a., fewr dahss Film-ine-lay-gen

14. Kinotechniker:
Kee-noh-tek-nik-er:

a. Luftaufnahme
Looft-owf-nah-meh

b. figürlicher Trick
fig-ewr-likh-er Trik

c. Dokumentarfilm
Doh-koo-men-tar-film

d. Reportagefilm/Wochenschau
Ray-pohr-tah-zheh-film/Voh-ken-sh'ow

e. Projektion (hinter oder vorn)
Proh-yehk-ts'yohn (hin-tehr oh-dehr fohrn)

f. zweites Team
tsvye-tehs Teh-ahm

g. Spezial Effekte
Shpayt-see-ahl Ay-fek-teh

h. Einergang
Eye-ner-gahng

Camera (continued):

14. Cinematographer (continued):

i. underwater

15. Still Photographer

16. Projectionist

17. Cinetechnician (camera repair person)

Cast:

18. Actor

19. Actress

20. Featured Player

21. Supporting Player

22. Bit Player

23. Stand-in

24. Extra

25. Stunt Person

Kamera (fortsetzung):
Kah-may-rah (fawrt-zet-soong):

14. Kinotechniker (Fortsetzung):
Kee-noh-tek-nik-er (fawrt-zet-soong):

i. unterwasser
oon-ter-vah-ser

15. Standfotograf
Shtahnt-foh-toh-grahf

16. (Film) Vorführer
(Film) For-f'yewr-er

17. Filmtechniker
Film-tek-nik-er

Besetzung:
Beh-zet-soong:

18. Schauspieler
Sh'ow-shpee-ler

19. Schauspielerin
Sh'ow-shpee-ler-in

20. Hauptdarsteller
Howpt-dar-shtell-er

21. Nebendarsteller
Nay-ben-dar-shtell-er

22. Kleindarsteller
Kline-dar-shteller

23. Doppel
Dop-p'l

24. Komparse/Statist
Kohm-par-zeh/Shtah-tist

25. Stunter
Shtoon-ter

Cast (continued):

26. Double

27. Man

28. Woman

29. Boy

30. Girl

31. Teacher

32. Welfare Worker

Directors:

33. Director

34. Dialogue Director

35. 1st Assistant Director

36. 2nd Assistant Director

37. Second Unit Director

38. Trainee

Besetzung (fortsetzung):
Beh-zet-soong (fawrt-zet-soong):

26. Doppelganger
Dop-p'l-gahng-er

27. Mann
Mahn

28. Frau
Fr'ow

29. Junge
Yoon-geh

30. Mädchen
Mayt-chen

31. Lehrer
Lay-rer

32. Sozialarbeiter
Sohlt-see-ahl-ar-bye-ter

Regie:
Reh-zhee:

33. Regisseur
Reh-zhee-suhr

34. Dialogregisseur
D'yah-lohg-reh-zhee-suhr

35. Erster Regieassistent
Ayr-ster Reh-zhee-ah-sis-stent

36. Zweiter Regieassistent
T'svye-ter Reh-zhee-ah-sis-stent

37. Regisseur des Zweiten Teams
Reh-zhee-suhr dess T'svye-ten-ah-sis-tent

38. Praktikant
Prahk-tee-kahnt

Editing:

39. Editor

40. 1st Assistant Editor

41. 2nd Assistant Editor

42. Sound Editor

43. Sound Effects Editor

44. Music Editor

45. Negative Cutter

46. Film Librarian

Electrical:

47. Gaffer

48. Assistant Gaffer

49. Best Boy

50. Best Girl

51 Electrician

Schnitt:
Shnitt:

39. Schnittmeister
Shnitt-my-ster

40. Erster Schnittassistent
Ayr-ster Shnitt-my-ster

41. Zweiter Schnittassistent
T'svye-ter Shnitt-my-ster

42. Ton-Schnittmeister
Tohn-Shnitt-my-ster

43. Schnittmeister für Toneffekte
Shnitt-my-ster fewr Tohn-eh-fek-teh

44. Schnittmeister für Musik
Shnitt-my-ster fewr Moo-zeek

45. Negativ-Schnittmeister
Nay-gah-teef-Shnitt-my-ster

46. Filmarchivar
Film-arkh-if-ar

Licht:
Likht:

47. Chefbeleuchter
Shef-beh-loykh-ter

48. Beleuchterassistent
Beh-loykh-ter-ah-sis-tent

49. Männliche Hilfskraft
Men-likh-eh Hilfs-krahft

50. Weibliche Hilfskraft
Vye-blikh-eh Hilfs-kraft

51. Elektriker
Eh-lek-trik-er

Electrical (continued):

52. Lamp Operator

53. Generator Operator

54. Cable Person

First Aid:

55. Doctor

56. Nurse

57. Paramedic

58. Attendant

Grip:

59. Key Grip

60. 1st Assistant Grip

61. Best Boy

62. Best Girl

63. Dolly Grip

Licht (fortsetzung):
Likht (fawrt-zet-soong):

52. Beleuchterassistent
    Beh-loykh-ter-ah-sis-tent

53. Bedienungsperson für den Generator
    Beh-dee-noongs-per-sohn fewr den Gen-eh-rah-tor

54. Kabelträger
    Kah-bel-tray-ger

Erste Hilfe:
Ayr-steh Hilf-eh:

55. Doktor/Arzt
    Dohk-tor/Artst

56. Krankenschwester
    Krahn-ken-shveh-ster

57. Sanitäter
    Sah-nih-tay-ter

58. (Hilfs-)Krankenpfleger
    (Hilfs-)Krahn-ken-pflay-ger

Atelierarbeiter:
Ah-tel-yehr-ar-bye-ter

59. Atelier-Vorarbeiter
    Ah-tell-yehr-For-ar-bye-ter

60. Atelier Arbeiterassistent
    Ah-tel-yehr Ar-bye-ter-ah-sis-tent

61. Männliche Hilfskraft
    Men-likh-eh Hilfs-krahft

62. Weibliche Hilfskraft
    Vye-blikh-eh Hilfs-krahft

63. Dollyfahrer
    Doh-lee-fah-rer

Grip (continued):

64. Crane Operator

65. Grip

66. Boom Operator

67. Rigger

Makeup:

68. Key Makeup Artist

69. Assistant Makeup Artist

70. Body Makeup Artist

71. Key Hairdresser

72. Hairdresser

73. Appliance Technician

Management:

74. Executive Producer

75. Producer

Atelierarbeiter (fortsetzung):
Ah-tel-yehr-ar-bye-ter (fawrt-zet-soong):

64. Kranfahrer
Krahn-fah-rer

65. Atelierarbeiter
Ah-tel-yehr-ar-bye-ter

66. Bumangler
Boom-ahng-ler

67. Takler
Tahk-ler

Maske:
Mah-skeh:

68. Erster Maskenbildner
Ayr-ster Mah-sken-bilt-ner

69. Maskenbildner-Assistent
Mah-sken-bilt-ner-Ah-sis-tent

70. Körper-Maskenbildner
Kuhr-per-Mah-sken-bilt-ner

71. Meister-Friseur
Mye-ster-Frih-zoor

72. Friseur
Frih-zoor

73. Geräte-Techniker
Geh-ray-teh-Tekh-nik-er

Management:
Mah-nahzh-ment:

74. Produktionsleiter
Proh-dook-ts'yohns-lye-ter

75. Produzent
Proh-doo-ts'ent

Management (continued):

76. Associate Producer

77. Production Manager

78. Unit Manager

79. Attorney

80. Publicist

81. Location Auditor

82. Accountant

83. Bookkeeper

84. Production Assistant

85. Secretary

Properties:

86. Property Master

87. Asistant Property Master

88. Greens Person

Management (fortsetzung):
Mah-nahzh-ment (fawrt-zet-soong):

76. Produktionsleiter
Proh-dook-ts'yohns-lye-ter

77. Aufnahmeleiter
Owf-nah-meh-lye-ter

78. Aufnahmeleiter
Owf-nah-meh-lye-ter

79. Rechtsanwalt
Rekht-sahn-vahlt

80. Pressesprecher/Publizist
Press-eh-shprek-er/Poo-blih-ts'ist

81. Rechnungsprüfer für Aussenaufnahmen
Rekh-noongs-prew-fer fewr Ows-sen-owf-nah-men

82. Buchhalter (qualifiziert)
Bookh-hahl-ter (kwah-lif-its-yehrt

83. Buchhalter
Bookh-hahl-ter

84. Produktionsassistent
Proh-dook-ts'yohn-ah-sis-tent

85. Sekretärin
Sek-reh-tayr-in

Requisiten:
Reh-kwih-zit-en

86. Requisiteur
Reh-kwih-zit-ewr

87. Assistent des Requisiteurs
Ah-sis-tent des Reh-kwih-zit-ewr

88. Gärtner
Gayrt-ner

Security:

89. Chief

90. Captain

91. Lieutenant

92. Inspector

93. Sergeant

94. Guard

95. Armed Guard

96. Police Officer

97. Special Officer

98. Motorcycle Officer

99. Vehicle Officer

100. Traffic Control Person

101. Police Escort

102. Military Escort

Sicherheitsdienst:
Zikh-er-hyts-deenst:

89. Vorgesetzter
For-geh-zets-ter

90. Hauptmann
Howpt-mahn

91. Leutnant
Loyt-nahnt

92. Inspektor
In-spek-tohr

93. Polizeimeister
Poh-lit-sye-mye-ster

94. Wächter/Wache
Vehkh-ter/Vahkh-eh

95. Bewaffneter Wächter
Beh-vahf-net-er Vekh-ter

96. Polizist
Poh-lit-sist

97. Polizist im Sondereinsatz
Poh-lit-sist ihm Zohn-der-eye'n-zahts

98. Motorradstreife
Moh-tohr-rahd-shtrye-feh

99. Funkstreifen-Polizist
Foonk-shtrye-fen-Poh-lit-sist

100. Verkehrspolizist
Fehr-kehs-poh-lit-sist

101. Polizeieskorte
Poh-lit-sye-ehs-kohr-teh

102. Militäreskorte
Mil-ih-tayr-ehs-kohrt-eh

Security (continued):

103. Soldier

104. Sailor

105. Marine

106. Coast Guard

107. Firefighter

Set Construction:

108. Supervising Set Builder

109. Supervisor

110. Foreman

111. Lead Person

112. Carpenter

113. Assistant Carpenter

114. Key Painter

115. Painter

Sicherheitsdienst (fortsetzung):
Zikh-er-hyts-deenst (fawrt-zet-soong):

103. Soldat
Zohl-daht

104. Seeman
Zee-mahn

105. Marineinfantrist
Mah-rin-eh-in-fahn-trist

106. Küstenwache
Kew-stehn-vahkh-eh

107. Feuerwehrmann
Foy-er-vehr-mahn

Bühnenbau:
Bew-nen-b'ow:

108. Leitender Filmarchitekt
Lye-ten-der Film-arkh-ih-tekt

109. Oberleiter
Oh-ber-lye-ter

110. Leitender Vorarbeiter
Lye-ten-der Fohr-ar-bye-ter

111. Vorarbeiter
Fohr-ar-bye-ter

112. Tischler/Zimmermann
Tish-ler/Ts'ihm-mer-mahn

113. Tischlergeselle
Tish-ler-geh-zel-eh

114. Leitender Maler
Lye-ten-der Mah-ler

115. Anstreicher/Maler
Ahn-shtrye-kher/Mah-ler

Set Construction (continued):

116. Sign Writer

117. Draper

118. Upholsterer

119. Paperhanger

120. Tiler

121. Plasterer

122. Plumber

123. Electrician

124. Model Builder

125. Prop Maker

Sound:

126. Mixer

127. Recordist

128. Boom Person

Bühnenbau (fortsetzung):
Bew-nen-b'ow (fawrt-zet-soong):

116. Schildermaler
Shil-ter-mah-ler

117. Drapierer
Drah-peer-er

118. Tapezierer
Tah-pet-seer-er

119. Weissbinder
Vyes-bint-er

120. Fliessenleger
Fleesen-lay-ger

121. Weissbinder
Vyes-bint-er

122. Installateur
In-stahl-lah-tewr

123. Elektriker
Eh-lek-trik-er

124. Modellbauer
Moh-del-b'ow-er

125. Ausstätter für Spezielle Aufgaben
Ows-shteht-ter fewr Shpet-s'yehl-eh Owf-gah-ben

TON:
Tohn:

126. Tonmeister (für die Mischung)
Tohn-mye-ster fewr dee Mih-shoong)

127. Toningenieur/Tonmeister
-in-zhen-yewr/Tohn-mye-ster

128. Mikrofon-assistent
Mik-roh-fohn-ah-sis-tent

Sound (continued):

129. Cable Person

130. Newsreel

131. Playback Operator

132. Re-recording Mixer

133. Music/Sound Effects Mixer

134. Maintenance Engineer

Transportation:

135. Driver Foreman

136. Chauffeur

137. Truck Driver

138. Camera Car

139. Stunt Car

140. Dispatcher

141. Mechanic

Ton (fortsetzung):
Tohn (fawrt-set-zoong):

129. Kabelträger
Kah-bel-tray-ger

130. Wochenschau
Vohkh-en-sh'ow

131. Tonmeister für Playback
Tohn-mye-ster fewr Play-bahk

132. Tonmeister für die Überspielung
Tohn-mye-ster fewr dee Ew-ber-shpeel-oong

133. Tonmeister für Musik und Geräusche
Tohn-mye-ster fewr Moo-zeek oont Geh-roy-sheh

134. Wartungs Ingnieur
Vahr-toongs In-zhen-ewr

Fahrdienst:
Fahr-deenst:

135. Fahrdienstleiter
Fahr-deenst-lye-ter

136. Chauffer
Sho-fer

137. Lastwagenfahrer
Lahst-vah-gen-fah-rer

138. Kamerawagen
Kah-may-rah-vah-gen

139. Stuntwagen
Shttont-vah-gen

140. Bote
Boh-teh

141. Mechaniker
Mekh-ah-nik-er

Video:

142. Technical Director

143. Lighting Director

144. Shader

145. Cameraperson

146. Tape Recordist

147. Kine Recordist

148. Telecine Operator

149. Audio Mixer

150. Public Address Operator

151. Floor Manager

152. Video Tape Operator

153. Engineer

154. Maintenance Engineer

155. Technical Coordinator

Video:
Vih-day-oh:

142. Technischer Regisseur
Tek-nish-er Reh-zhih-sewr

143. Lichtregisseur
Likht-reh-zhih-sewr

144. Farbabstufungen und Schattierung Techniker
Far-bahb-shtoo-foon-gen oont Shaht-eer-oong Tekh-nik-er

145. Kameramann
Kah-may-rah-mahn

146. Bandmeister
Bahnt-mye-ster

147. Filmaufzeichner (FAZ)
Film-owf-ts'eyekh-ner (Ef-Ah-Ts'et)

148. Bedienungsperson für den Filmabtaster
Beh-deen-oongs-pehr-sohn fewr den Film-ahp-tahs-ter

149. Tonmischer
Tohn-mish-er

150. Bedienungsperson für die Beschallungsanlage
Beh-deen-oongs-pehr-sohn fewr dee Beh-shahl-loong-sahn-lah-geh

151. Aufnahmeleiter
Owf-nah-meh-lye-ter

152. Videotechniker
Vih-day-oh-tek-nik-er

153. Ingenieur
In-zhen-ewr

154. Messingenieur
Mehs-in-zhen-ewr

155. Technischer Koordinator
Tek-nish-er Koh-ohr-dih-nah-tohr

Video (continued):

156. Associate Director

157. Cue Card Person

158. Cable Person

159. Switcher (Vision Mixer)

WARDROBE:

160. Key Wardrobe

161. Assistant Wardrobe

162. Costumer

163. Dresser

164. Fitter

165. Tailor

Video (fortsetzung):
Vih-day-oh (fawrt-zet-soong):

156. Co-regisseur
Koh-reh-zhih-sewr

157. Stichwortgeber (mit Karten)
Shtikh-vort-geh-ber (mit Kar-ten)

158. Kabelträger
Kah-bel-tray-ger

159. Bildmischer
Bilt-mish-er

Kostümfundus:
Kah-st'yewm-foon-doos:

160. Gewandmeister
Geh-vahnt-mye-ster

161. Assistent des Gewandmeister
Ah-sis-tent dehs Geh-vahnt-mye-ster

162. Kostümierer
Kah-st'yewm-yehr-er

163. Garderobiere
Gahr-deh-roh-b'yehr-eh

164. Schneider
Shnye-der

165. Schneider
Shnye-der

01. Ready

02. Silence

03. Roll camera

04. Roll tape

05. Speed!

06. Slate

07. Mark it!

08. One moment

09. Action!

10. Cut

11. Print it

12. How was that?

13. Good take

14. No good

15. Fair

NÜTZLICHE WORTE & REDEWENDUNGEN AM DREHPLATZ 15

NOOTS-LIKH-EH VORT-EH & RAY-DEH-VEND-OON-GEN AHM DRAY-PLAHTS

01. Fertig
Fehr-tik

02. Ruhe
Roo-eh

03. Kamera ab
Kah-may-rah ahp

04. Ton ab
Tohn ahp

05. Geschwindigkeit
Gehsh-vint-ik-kyte

06. Klappe/Szenentafel
Klahp-peh/Stsen-en-tah-fel

07. Kennzeichnen!
Ken-tsye-kh'nen!

08. Einen Augenblick
Eye'n-en Ow-gen-blik

09. Action
Ahk-ts'yohn

10. Scnitt
Shnitt

11. Wird kopiert (K)
Veert koh-peert

12. Wie war das?
Vee var dahs?

13. Gute Aufnahme
Goot-eh Owf-nah-meh

14. Nicht gute
Nikht goot-eh

15. Soso/Mittelprächtig
Zoh-zoh/Mit-tel-prekh-tik

16. Excellent

17. Missed the mark

18. Missed the cue

19. Too early

20. Too late

21. Once more

22. Clear (the view of) camera

23. What is next?

24. Another angle

25. Another set-up

26. Our next shot is -- .

27. A ______ shot:

 a. dolly

 b. crane

 c. lockdown

16. Wunderbar/Ausgezeichnet
Voon-der-bar/Ows-geht-sye-khnet

17. Markierung verfehlt
Mar-kee-roong fehr-fehlt

18. Einsatz verpasst
Eye'n-zahts fehr-pahst

19. Zu früh
Tsoo frew

20. Zu spät
Tsoo shpayt

21. Noch einmal
Nokh eye'n-mahl

22. Bitte aus dem Bild gehen
Bit-eh ows daym Bilt gay-en

23. Was kommt als nächstes?
Vahss kohmt ahls nekh-stehs?

24. Ein anderer Blickwinkel
Eye'n ahn-deh-rer Blik-vin-kel

25. Eine andere Szene
Eye'n ahn-deh-reh Stsen-eh

26. Unsere nächste Einstellen ist
Oon-seh-reh nekh-steh Eye'n-shtellen ihst

27. Eine ___ Einstellung:
Eye'neh ___ Eye'n-shtel-loong:

   a. Dolly/Kamerawagen
   Doh-lee/Kah-may-rah-vah-gen

   b. Kran
   Krahn

   c. Blockierung/Verriegelung
   Blohk-eer-oong/Fehr-ree-geh-loong

28. Lay down dolly:

    a. boards

    b. track

29. Start here

30. End there

31. Start there

32. End here

33. How long will it take?

34. How much time do we have?

35. When will this be ready?

36. I do not know

37. Who knows?

38. There will be a short delay

39. Why the delay?

40. There is a need for...

28. Abgestellter Kamerawagen:
Ahp-geh-shtel-ter Kah-may-rah-vah-gen:

    a. Holzklötze
    Holts-kluht-seh

    b. Shiene
    Shee-neh

29. Beginne hier
Beh-ginn-eh heer

30. Beende es dort
Beh-en-deh ess dohrt

31. Beginne dort
Beh-ginn-eh dohrt

32. Beende hier
Beh-en-deh heer

33. Wie lange wird das dauern?
Vee lahng-eh veert dahss dow-ern?

34. Wievel Zeit haben wir?
Vee-fel Tsye't hah-ben veer?

35. Wann wird das fertig sein?
Vahn veert dahss fehr-tik z'eye'n?

36. Ich weiss nicht
Ikh vise nikht

37. Wer weiss es?
Vehr vise ehss?

38. Es wird eine kurze Unterbrechnung geben
Ehss veert eye'neh koort-seh Oon-ter-brekh-noong gay-ben

39. Warum diese Unterbrechnung?
Vah-room dee-zeh Oon-ter-brekh-noong?

40. Wir brauchen______
Veer br'owkh-en ___

41. Adjusting a light

42. Waiting for the sun

43. Light them up! (luminaires)

44. Shake them up! (reflectors)

45. Ready for the actors

46. On stage

47. On location

48. Anytime you are ready

49. With your permission

50. Check makeup

51. Check hair

52. Check costume

53. Too much

54. Not enough

55. More

41. Licht einstellen
Likht eye'n-shtell-en

42. Auf die Sonne warten
Owf dee Zohn-neh var-ten

43. Licht an!
Likht ahn!

44. Reflektoren einrichten!
Reh-flek-toh-ren eye'n-rikh-ten!

45. Schauspieler bereitmachen
Sh'ow-shpee-ler beh-rye't-mahkh-en

46. Im Atelier
Ihm Ah-tel-yehr

47. Am Drehort
Ahm Dray-ahrt

48. Wenn Sie so weit sind
Ven Zee zo vite zint

49. Mit Ihrer Erlaubnis
Mit Eer-er Ehr-l'owp-nis

50. Überprüft das Maske
Ew-behr-prewft dahss Mah-skeh

51. Überprüft die Frisur
Ew-behr-prewft dee Frih-zoor

52. Überprüft das Kostüm
Ew-behr-prewft dahss Kah-st'yewm

53. Zu viel
Tsoo feel

54. Nicht genug
Nikht geh-nook

55. Mehr
Mehr

56. Less

57. Yes

58. No

59. Perhaps

60. Who

61. What

62. Where

63. Why

64. When

65. Tall

66. Long

67. Short

68. Squat

69. Help

70. Push

56. Weniger
Vay-nih-ger

57. Ja
Yah

58. Nein
Nine

59. Vielleicht
Feel-lye'kht

60. Wer
Vehr

61. Was
Wahss

62. Wo
Voh

63. Warum
Vah-room

64. Wann
Vahn

65. Hoch/Gross
Hohkh/Grohss

66. Lang
Lahng

67. Kurz
Koorts

68. Gedrungen
Geh-droon-gen

69. Hilfe
Hil-feh

70. Schieben
Shee-ben

71. Pull

72. Wait

73. Now

74. Slower

75. Faster

76. Attention everyone!

77. Wrong set

78. Wrong location

79. It's a move

80. Breakfast

81. Lunch

82. Dinner

83. Take a break

84. Where is the bathroom?

85. We are finished for today

71. Ziehen
Tsee-en

72. Warten
Vahr-ten

73. Jetzt/Nun
Yetst/Noon

74. Langsamer
Lahng-zahm-er

75. Schneller
Shnell-er

76. Achtung!
Ahkh-toong!

77. Falsches Atelier
Fahl-shes Ah-tel-yehr

78. Falscher Drehort
Fahl-sher Dray-ahrt

79. Drehplatzwechsel
Dray-plahts-vekh-sel

80. Früstück
Frew-shtewk

81. Mittagessen
Mit-tahk-ess-en

82. Abendessen
Ah-bent-ess-en

83. Eine Pause machen
Eye-neh Pow-zeh mahkh-en

84. Wo ist die Toilette?
Voh isst dee Taw-ah-let-eh?

85. Wir sind für heute fertig
Veer zint fewr hoy-teh fehr-tik

86. Crew call for tomorrow is...

87. Same time tomorrow

88. Different time tomorrow

89. Check the schedule

90. Weather permitting

91. When we start again...

92. I would like to see...

93. Would it be possible?

94. Anything you want

95. How soon?

96. All it takes is time and money

97. The most important words

    on any set are:

 a. Please

 b. Thank you

86. Arbeitsbeginn ist morgen um...
Ahr-bites-beh-gihn isst mor-gen oom.

87. Morgen zur gleichen Zeit
Mor-gen tsoor glye-khen Ts'eye't

88. Morgen zu einer anderen Zeit
Mor-gen tsoo eye'ner ahn-deh-ren Ts'eye't

89. Schauen Sie im Drehplan nach
Sh'ow-en Zee ihm Dray-plahn nahkh

90. Falls das Wetter es zulässt
Fahls dahs Vet-ter ehss tsoo-lest

91. Wann fangen wir wieder an...
Vahn fahn-gen veer vee-der ahn...

92. Ich würde gerne...sehen
Ikh vuhr-deh gayrn-eh...zay-en

93. Wäre es möglich...?
Vehr-meh ehs muh-glikh...?

94. Alles was du willst
Ahl-les wahss doo vihlst

95. Wie bald?
Vee bahlt?

96. Es braucht nur Zeit und Geld
Ehs br'owkht noor Tsite oont Gelt

97. ANMERKUNG: Die wichtigsten
AHN-MEHR-KOONG: Dee vik-tik-shten

Wörter an Jedem Drehort sind:
Vuhr-ter ahn Yay-dem Dray-hort zint:

a. Bitte
Bit-teh

b. Danke
Dahn-keh

01. Aperture

02. Aperture Plate

03. Barney

04. Battery

05. Black Bag

06. Blimp

07. Body Brace

08. Buckle-trip

09. Cable

10. Camera:

a. base

b. grease

c. oil

d. report

e. tape

KAMERA
KAH-MAY-RAH

01. Öffnung/Bildfenster
    Uhf-noong/Bilt-fehn-ster

02. Bildfensterplatte
    Bilt-fehn-ster-plaht-teh

03. Weicher Schall
    Vye-kher Shahl

04. Batterie
    Baht-teh-ree

05. Schwarzer Sack
    Shvahrts-er Zahk

06. Schallschutzhaube
    Shahl-shoots-how-beh

07. Körperstativ
    Kuhr-per-shtah-tif

08. Automatisch Ausschalten
    Ow-toh-mah-tish Ows-shahl-ten

09. Kabel
    Kah-bel

10. Kamera:
    Kah-may-rah:

    a. Boden
       Boh-den

    b. Fett
       Feht

    c. Öl
       Uhl

    d. bericht
       beh-rikt

    e. Band
       Bahnt

11. Changing Bag.

12. Close-up

13. Composition

14. Counter:

    a. digital

    b. light emitting diode (LED)

15. Darkroom

16. Darkroom Load

17. Day Filming

18. Day-For-Night

19. Daylight Load

20. Depth Of Field

21. Depth Of Focus

22. Diopter (lens)

23. Ditty Bag

11. Wechselsack
Vekh-sel-sahk

12. Nahaufnahme/Naheinstellung
Nah-owf-nah-meh/Nah-eye'n-shtel-loong

13. Bildaufbau
Bilt-owf-b'ow

14. Zähler/Zalwerk:
Tsay-ler/Tsahl-vehrk:

   a. digital
   dih-zhih-tahl

   b. Leuchtdiode
   Loykht-dih-oh-deh

15. Dunkelkammer
Doon-kel-kah-mer

16. Einlegen in der Dunkelkammer
Eye'n-lay-gen ihn dehr Doon-kel-kah-mer

17. Tageslichtaufnahme
Tahk-eh-shlikht-owf-nah-meh

18. amerikanische Nacht
ah-may-rih-kah-nish Nahkht

19. Einlegen bei Tageslicht
Eye'n-lay-gen by Tahk-eh-shlikht

20. Tiefenschärfe
Teef-en-shehrf-eh

21. Fokustiefe
Foh-koos-teef-eh

22. Dioptrie
Dih-ohp-tree

23. kleiner Zubehörbehälter
kly-ner Tsoo-beh-huhr-beh-hell-ter

24. Dolly Shot

25. Eyepiece

26. Exterior

27. Fast

28. Film jam

29. Filter:

 a. conversion

 b. graduated

 c. neutral density

 d. polarizing

 e. sky

 f. star

 g. fog

 h. fluorescent

30. Filter Holder

24. Kamerafahrt
Kah-may-rah-fahrt

25. Kameralupe/Okular
Kah-may-rah-loop-eh/Oh-koo-lahr

26. Aussenaufnahme
Ows-sen-owf-nah-meh

27. Schnell
Shnell

28. Filmsalat
Film-sah-laht

29. Filter:
Fil-ter

a. Konversions-
Kohn-vehr-z'yohns-

b. Verlauf-
Fehr-l'owf-

c. Neutralgrau-
Noy-trahl-gr'ow-

d. Polarisations-
Poh-lah-rih-zaht-s'yohns-

e. verlaufende-
fehr-l'owf-en-deh-

f. Star-
Shtar-

g. Schleier-
Shly-er-

h. fluoreszierend
floo-oh-rez-tsee-rent

30. Filterhalter
Fil-ter-hahl-ter

31. Flare

32. Focus:

a. follow-

b. -knob

c. mark

d. out-of-

e. sharp

33. Follow Shot

34. Frame

35. Frameline

36. Frames Per Second (fps)

37. Gate

38. Gear

39. Hair-check

40. High Angle

31. Überstrahlung
Ew-ber-shtrah-loong

32. Fokus:
Foh-koos:

a. Verfolgungsaufnahme-
Fehr-fahl-goongs-nah-meh-

b. Schärferad
Shehrf-eh-raht

c. Schärfezeichen
Shehrf-eht-s'eye-khen

d. unscharf
oon-shahrf

e. scharf
shahrf

33. Verfolgunsaufnahme
Fehr-fohl-goons-owf-nah-meh

34. Bildfeld
Bilt-felt

35. Bildstrich
Bilt-shtrik

36. Bilder pro Sekunde
Bilt-er proh Zeh-koon-deh

37. Bildfenster
Bilt-fen-ster

38. Getriebe
Geh-tree-beh

39. Fusselkontrolle
Foos-sell-kohn-troh-leh

40. hohe Bildwinkel
ho-eh Bilt-vin-kel

41. Hold

42. Insert

43. Interior

44. Intermittant

45. Lens

46. Lens Cleaner

47. Lens Mount

48. Level

49. Lockdown Screw

50. Long Shot

51. Low Angle

52. Magazine:

  a. co-axial

  b. displacement

  c. feed side

41. Spar es auf
Shpahr ehss owf

42. Insert
In-zehrt

43. Innenaufnahme
In-nen-owf-nah-meh

44. Zeitraffer
Ts'eye-trahf-er

45. Linse
Linz-eh

46. Linsenreiniger
Linz-en-rye-nig-er

47. Objektivfassung
Ahp-yek-teef-fahs-soong

48. Pegel
Pay-gel

49. Feststellschraube
Fehst-shtel-shr'ow-beh

50. Fernaufnahme
Fehrn-owf-nah-meh

51. niedriger Winkel
nee-drih-ger Vin-kel

52. Kassette:
Kah-set-eh:

a. konzentrisch
kohnt-sen-trish

b. Verschiebung
Fehr-shee-boong

c. Abwickelseite
Ahp-vik-el-z'eye-teh

52. Magazine (continued):

d. lid

e. lighttrap

f. spindle wheel

g. take-up side

h. throat

53. Masking Tape

54. Matte

55. Matte-box

56. Medium Shot

57. Meter:

a. incident

b. reflectance

c. spot

d. color temperature

52. Kassette (fortsetzung):
Kah-set-eh (fawrt-zet-soong):

d. Deckel
Dek-el

e. Lichtschleuse
Likht-shloy-zeh

f. Spindelrad
Shpin-del-raht

g. Aufwickelseite
Owf-vik-el-zite-eh

h. Hals
Hahls

53. Abdeckband
Ahp-dek-bahnt

54. Maske
Mahsk-eh

55. Kompendium
Kahm-pen-d'yoom

56. Halbnah
Hahlp-nah

57. Belichtungmesser:
Beh-likh-toongs-messer:

a. einfallend
eye'n-fahl-ent

b. Reflectiert
Ray-flek-teert

c. Partialbelichtungmesser
Part-s'yahl-beh-likh-toong-mess-er

d. Farbtemperatur
Farb-tem-pehr-ah-toor

58. Motion Picture Camera

59. Motor:

a. animation

b. crystal-controlled

c. time-lapse

d. intermittant

e. slow-motion

f. high-speed

g. very-high-speed

h. ultra-high-speed

60. Movement:

a. pulldown claw

b. registration-pin

61. Night Filming

62. On/Off Switch

58. Filmkamera
Film-kah-may-rah

59. Motor:
Moh-ter:

a. Trick
Trik

b. quartzgesteuert
kvahrts-geh-shtoy-ert

c. Zeitraffer
Ts'eye-trahf-er

d. intermitterend
in-tehr-mitt-er-rent

e. Zeitlupe
Tsite-loop-eh

f. Zeitdehner
Tsite-deh-ner

g. extreme Zeitdehnung
eks-tray-meh Tsite-deh-noong

h. ultra Zeitdehnung
ool-tra Tsite-deh-noong

60. Bewegung:
Beh-vek-oong:

a., Greifer
Gry-fer

b. Sperrgreifer
Shpehr-gry-fer

61. Nachtaufnahme
Nakht-owf-nah-meh

62. An- und Ausschalter
Ahn- oont Ows-shahl-ter

63. Over-the-shoulder

64. Pan:

a. left

b. right

65. Pan Handle

66. Pan Lock

67. Parallax

68. Periscope Finder

69. Pressure-pad

70. Printed Take

71. Process Shot:

a. blue screen

b. front projection

c. rear projection

d. traveling-matte

63. Über die Schulter
Ew-ber dee Shool-ter

64. Panorama (Schwenk):
Pah-noh-rah-mah (Shvenk):

a. links
links

b. rechts
rekts

65. Schwenkarm
Shvenk-ahrm

66. Schwenkschloss
Shvenk-shlohss

67. Parallaxe
Pah-rah-lahks-eh

68. Periskopsucher
Pehr-ih-skohp-zoo-kher

69. Andruckkufe (am Bildfenster)
Ahn-drook-koo-feh (ahm Bilt-fen-ster)

70. Kopierte Einstellung
Koh-peer-teh Eye'n-shtel-loong

71. Kombinationsaufnahme:
Kohm-bin-aht-s'yohn-owf-nah-meh:

a. Blaustanzverfahren
Bl'ow-shtahnts-fehr-fah-ren

b. Aufprojektion
Owf-proh-yekt-s'yohn

c. Rückprojektion
Rewk-proh-yekt-s'yohn

d. Wandermaske
Vahn-der-mah-skeh

72. Rackover

73. Receptacle

74. Re-load

75. Re-take

76. Reverse Angle

77. Roller

78. Safe-action-area

79. Shipping label

80. Shoulder-pod

81. Shutter:

a. fixed

b. variable

c. mirror-reflex

d. butterfly

e. open-segment

72. Verschieden die Kamera
Fehr-shee-den dee Kah-may-rah

73. Behälter
Beh-hel-ter

74. Nachladen
Nahkh-lah-den

75. Wiederholung
Vee-der-hoh-loong

76. Gegenschuss
Geh-gen-shlooss

77. Rolle
Rohl-leh

78. Sicherheitzone
Zikh-er-hite-tsoh-neh

79. Versande Tikett
Fehr-zahnt-eh Tik-ett

80. Schulterstativ
Shool-ter-shtah-teef

81. Verschluss:
Fehr-shlooss:

a. fixiert
fiks-eert

b. variabel
vahr-yah-bel

c. Spiegelreflex
Shpee-gel-ray-fleks

d. Schmetterling
Shmeht-tehr-ling

e. Blendenausschnitt
Blen-den-owss-shnitt

82. Sequence

83. Slate

84. Spreader

85. Speed:

a. fast

b. slow

c. high

d. synchronous

e. variable

86. Sprocket

87. Still Camera

88. Stop (lens)

89. Stop (camera)

90. Tachometer

91. Take

KAMERA (fort.)
KAH-MAY-RAH (fawrt.)

82. Sequenz
Zay-kvents

83. Klappe
Klah-peh

84. Spreizfuss
Shpryts-fooss

85. Geschwindigkeit:
Geh-shvint-ik-kite:

a. schnell
shnell

b. langsam
lahng-zahm

c. hoch-
hohkh-

d. synchron
zewn-krohn

e. variabel
vahr-y'ah-bel

86. Filmzahnrolle
Film-tsahn-roh-leh

87. Standbiltkamera
Shtahnt-bilt-kah-may-rah

88. Blende
Blen-deh

89. Stillstand
Shtill-shtant

90. Tachometer
Tahks-oh-may-ter

91. Aufnahme/Take
Owf-nah-meh/Tayk

92. Take-up

93. Take-up Belt

94. Telephoto

95. Test

96. Threading

97. Three-shot

98. Tie-down Chain

99. Tilt:

a. down

b. up

100. Tilt Plate

101. Timing Gear

102. Turret

103. Tripod:

a. standard legs

92. Aufwickeln
Owf-vik-ehln

93. Aufwickelriemen
Owf-vik-ehl-ree-men

94. Teleaufnahme
Tay-lay-owf-nah-meh

95. Test
Test

96. Filmeinlegen
Film-eye'n-lay-gen

97. Aufnahme mit drei Darstellern
Owf-nah-me mitt dry Dahr-shtell-ern

98. Stativ Anketten
Shtah-tif Ahn-keht-ten

99. Neigung:
Nye-goong:

a. nach unten
nakh oon-ten

b. nach oben
nakh oh-ben

100. Neigeplatte
Nye-geh-plaht-teh

101. Laufzeitmesser
L'owf-tsite-mess-er

102. Revolverkopf
Reh-vahl-vehr-kuhpf

103. Stativ:
Shtah-tif:

a. Normalhöhe
Nor-mahl-huh-eh

103. Tripod (cont):

b. medium legs

c. baby legs

d. hi-hat

104. Tripod Handle

105. Tripod Head:

a. slip

b. fluid

c. geared

106. Tripod Parts:

a. legs

b. shoe

c. point

d. spur

e. adjusting knobs

103. Stativ (fortsetzung):
Shtah-tif (fawrt-zet-soong):

b. mittlere Höhe
mit-leh-reh Huh-eh

c. Baby-
Bah-bee-

d. -kopfaufsatz
-kupf-owf-zahts

104. Stativ-Griff
Shtah-tif-Grif

105. Stativkopf:
Shtah-tif-kupf:

a. Friktions
Frik-ts'yohns

b. flüssig
flew-sik

c. mit Zahnradübersetzung
mit Tsahn-rahd-ew-ber-zet-soong

106. Stativ-Teile:
Shtah-tif-Tye-leh:

a. Füsse
Few-seh

b. Fussschutz
Fooss-shoots

c. Spitze
Shpit-seh

d. Sporn
Shporn

e. Feststellschrauben
Feh-shtell-shr'ow-ben

107. Two-shot

108. Viewfinder:

   a. reflex

   b. offset

109. Wide-angle

110. Zoom Shot

Useful Terms:

111. Exposed Film

112. Raw Stock

113. Short End

114. Ship Air Express

115. Special Handling

116. Airbill Number

117. Waybill number

118. Packing Slip Enclosed

107. Fahraufnahme
Fahr-owf-nah-meh

108. Sucher:
Zoo-kher:

a. Reflex-
Ray-fleks-

b. Ausgleichen-
Ows-glye-khen-

109. Weitwinkel
Vite-vin-kel

110. Zoom-Aufnahme
Tsoom-Owf-nah-meh

Nützliche Begriffe:
Newt-slikh-eh Beh-grif-eh:

111. Entwickelter Film
Ent-vik-elt-er Film

112. Rohfilm
Roh-film

113. Rollenende
Rohl-en-en-deh

114. Versand Luftracht
Fehr-zahnt Looft-rahkht

115. Express Zustellung
Eks-press Tsoo-shtel-loong

116. Luftfrachtnummer
Looft-frahkht-noo-mer

117. Frachtnummer
Frahkht-noo-mer

118. Lieferschein Einliegend
Lee-fehr-shine Eye'n-lee-gehnt

01. Advanced Sync

02. Background

03. Bench

04. Bin

05. Black-and-White (B&W):

a. film

b. negative

c. original

d. print

e. reversal

06. Blow-up

07. Cement

08. Cleaner

09. Coding

SCHNITT
SHNITT

01. Bild/Ton-Versatz
Bilt/Tohn-Fehr-zahts

02. Hintergrund
Hin-ter-groont

03. Bank
Bahnk

04. Abfalleimer
Ahp-fahl-eye-mer

05. Schwarz und Weiss (s/w)
Shvarts oont Vice (ess oont vay)

a. film
film

b. negativ
nay-gah-teef

c. original
oh-rih-gih-nahl

d. kopie
koh-pee

e. umkehr
oom-kehr

06. Blow-up
Bloh-oop

07. Filmkitt
Film-kit

08. Reiniger
Rye-nig-er

09. Kodieren
Koh-deer-en

10. Color:

a. film

b. negative

c. original

d. print

e. reversal

11. Composite Daily

12. Counter:

a. footage

b. metric

c. digital

d. light emitting diode (LED)

13. Credits

14. Cut

15. Cutter

10. Farbe:
Fahr-beh:

a. -film
-film

b. negativ
nay-gah-teef

c. original
oh-rih-gih-nahl

d. kopie
koh-pee

e. umkehr
oom-kehr

11. Kombiniertes Muster
Kohm-bin-eer-tehs Moo-ster

12. Zähler:
Tseh-ler:

a. filmlange
film-lahng-eh

b. metrisch
met-rish

c. digital
dih-zhih-tahl

d. Leuchtdiode
Loykht-dih-oh-deh

13. Titelvorspann
Tih-tel-for-shpahn

14. Schnitt
Shnitt

15. Cutter/Cutterin
Coo-ter/Coo-ter-in

16. Dailies

17. Dead Sync

18. Edge-number

19. Editing Machine:

   a. flat bed

   b. upright

20. Editorial Process

21. Editorial Sync

22. Fade-in

23. Fade-out

24. Fine Cut

25. Fine Grain

26. Frame

27. Frameline

28. Frameline Dirt

16. Muster
Moo-ster

17. Fertige Synchronisation
Fehr-tik-eh Zewn-kroh-nih-zaht-s'yohn

18. Fussnummer
Foos-noo-mer

19. Schneidetisch:
Shnye-deh-tish:

  a. horizontaler-
  haw-rit-sohn-tahl-er

  b. hochformatiger
  hokh-fawr-mah-tik-er

20. Filmschnitt
Film-shnitt

21. Schnittsynchron
Shnitt-zewn-krohn

22. Aufblende
Owf-blen-deh

23. Abblende
Ahp-blen-deh

24. Feinschnitt
Fine-shnitt

25. Feinkorn
Fine-kawrn

26. Bildfeld
Bilt-felt

27. Bildstrich
Bilt-shtrikh

28. Schmutz auf dem Bildstrich
Shmoots owf dem Bilt-shtrikh

29. Intercut

30. Interlock

31. Laboratory

32. Lab Report

33. Leader:

   a. academy

   b. black

   c. clear

   d. colored

   e. filler

   f. opaque

   g. white

34. Light Box

35. Magnetic

36. Marking Pen

29. Zwischenschnitt
Tsvih-shen-shnitt

30. Interlock
In-tehr-lohk

31. Kopierwerk
Koh-peer-vehrk

32. Kopierwerksbericht
Koh-peer-vehrks-beh-rikt

33. Vorspann/Startband:
For-shpann/Shtahrt-bahnt:

a. Vorspann nach Hollywood-standard
Fohr-shpann nahkh Hah-lee-voot-Shtahn-dart

b. schwarz
shvahrts

c. klar
klahr

d. farbig
fahr-bik

e. Füllmaterial
Fewl-mah-tehr-ee-ahl

f. milchig
milkh-ik

g. weiss
vice

34. Lichtkasten
Likht-kah-sten

35. Magnetisch
Mahg-neh-tish

36. Markierstift
Mar-keer-shtift

37. Negative Scratch

38. Optical Sound

39. Out-takes

40. Picture

41. Positive Scratch

42. Print:

a. answer-

b. contact-

c. one-light-

d. optical-

e. preview-

f. release

g. timed-

h. trailer

i. work-

37. Kratzer auf dem Negativ
    Kraht-ser owf dem Nay-gah-teef

38. Lichton
    Likh-tohn

39. Schnittreste
    Shnitt-reh-steh

40. Bild/Aufnahme
    Bilt/Owf-nah-meh

41. Kratzer auf dem Positiv
    Kraht-ser owf dem Poh-zih-teef

42. Kopie:
    Koh-pee:

    a. Erst-
       Ayrst-

    b. Kontakt-
       Kohn-tahkt

    c. Einlicht-
       Eye'n-likht-

    d. optisches Kopieren
       ohp-tish-es Koh-peer-en

    e. Abnahme-
       Ahp-nah-meh-

    f. Massen-/Vorführ-
       Mahs-sehn-/Fohr-fewr-

    g. lichtbestimmte-
       likht-beh-shtim-teh-

    h. Vorspann/Trailer
       Fohr-shpahn/Trah-ih-ler

    i. Arbeits-
       Ahr-bites-

43. Printed Takes

44. Print Down

45. Print Up

46. Razor Blade

47. Reader:

   a. magnetic

   b. optical

48. Reduction

49. Reel:

   a. split-

50. Retarded Sync

51. Rewind (noun)

52. Re-wind (verb)

53. Rough Cut

54. Scene

43. Kopierte Einstellungen
Koh-peer-teh Eye'n-shtell-oon-gen

44. Dunkeln
Doon-keln

45. Erhellen
Ehr-hell-en

46. Rasierklinge
Rah-seer-klin-geh

47. Tonkopf:
Tohn-kupf:

a. magnetisch
mahg-neh-tish

b. optisch
ohp-tish

48. Verkleinerung
Fehr-kline-eh-roong

49. Rolle/Spule:
Rohl-leh/Shpoo-leh:

a. zerlegbare
tsehr-lehg-bah-reh

50. verzögerte Synchronität
fehrt-suh-gehr-teh Zewn-kroh-nih-teht

51. Rückspulen
Rewk-shpool-en

52. umrollen
oom-rohl-en

53. Rohschnitt
Roh-shnitt

54. Szene
Stsay-neh

55. Scissors

56. Scraper

57. Sealing Tape

58. Sequence

59. Shot-size:

a. close-up

b. extreme close-up

c. extreme long shot

d. insert

e. long shot

f. medium shot

g. over-the-shoulder

h. telephoto

i. three-shot

j. two-shot

55. Schere
Shay-reh

56. Schabemesser
Shah-beh-mess-er

57. Klebeband
Klay-beh-bahnt

58. Sequenz
Zay-kvents

59. Einstellungen:
Eye'n-shtel-loon-gen:

a. Nahaufnahme
Nah-owf-nah-meh

b. Grossaufnahme
Grohs-owf-nah-meh

c. extreme Totale
eks-tray-meh Toh-tahl-eh

d. Zwischenschnitt
Tsvih-shen-shnitt

e. Totale
Toh-tahl-eh

f. halbnah
hahlp-nah

g. über-schulter-aufnahme
ew-ber-shool-ter-owf-nah-meh

h. Fernaufnahme
Fehrn-owf-nah-meh

i. Dreieraufnahme
Dry-er-owf-nah-meh

j. Zweieraufnahme
T svy-er-owf-nah-meh

60. Silent

61. Sound

62. Sound Tape

63. Sound Track:

a. composite

b. dialogue

c. effect

d. music

e. narration

f. optical

64. Splice:

a. bevel

b. overlap

c. straight

d. taped

60. Ruhe
Roo-eh

61. Ton
Tohn

62. Tonband
Tohn-bahnt

63. Tonspur:
Tohn-shpoor

a. kombinierte
kohm-bin-eer-teh

b. dialog-
dee-ah-lohg-

c. effekte-
eh-fek-teh-

d. Musik-
Moo-zeek-

e. Sprachtext-
Shprahk-tekst-

f. optische
ohp-tish-eh

64. Klebestelle:
Klay-beh-shtell-eh:

a. schräg
shrek

b. überlappen
ew-ber-lahp-en

c. gerade
geh-rahd-eh

d. geklebt
geh-klept

65. Splicer:

  a. butt

  b. cold

  c. hot

66. Splicing Tape:

  a. clear

  b. color

  c. white

67. Synchronizer

68. Sync mark

69. Timing

70. Titles

71. Transfer

72. Trims

73. Viewer

65. Klebepresse:
Klay-beh-press-eh:

a. stumpf
shtoompf

b. kalt
kahlt

c. heiss
hye-ss

66. Klebeband:
Klay-beh-bahnt:

a. klar
klar

b. farbig
fahr-bik

c. weiss
vice

67. Synchronisator
Zewn-kroh-nih-zah-tor

68. Synchronmarke
Zewn-krohn-mahr-keh

69. Lichtbestimmung
Likht-beh-shtim-moong

70. Titel
Tih-tel

71. Überspielung
Ew-ber-shpee-loong

72. Schnittmaterial
Shnitt-mah-teh-rih-el

73. Betrachter
Beh-trahkh-ter

74. Visual Effects:

a. cut

b. dissolve

c. fade-in

d. fade-out

e. slow cut

f. split-screen

g. sub-title

h. superimpose

i. wipe

75. Voice-over

Useful Terms:

76. Do not project!

77. Pick Up From The Laboratory

78. Ready For Sound Mix

74. Optische Effekte:
Ohp-tish-eh Eh-fek-teh:

a. Schnitt
Snitt

b. Überblendung
Ew-behr-blen-doong

c. Aufblende
Owf-blen-deh

d. Abblende
Ahp-blen-deh

e. Langsam Schnitt
lahng-zahm Shnitt

f. geteiltes Bild
geh-tile-tehs Bilt

g. Untertitel
Oon-ter-tih-tel

h. Doppelbelichtet
dop-p'l-beh-likh-tet

i. Trickblende
Trik-blen-deh

75. Off-Kommentar
Ohf-Koh-men-tahr

Nützliche Begriffe:
Newt-slikh-eh Beh-griff-eh:

76. Nicht Projizieren!
Nikht Proh-yit-seer-en!

77. Vom Kopierwerk Abholen
Fom Koh-peer-vehrk Ahp-hoh-len

78. Fertig Zur Tonmischung
Fehr-tik Tsoor Tohn-mish-oong

Useful Terms (continued):

79. Scene Missing

80. Send To Laboratory

81. To Be Coded

Nützliche Begriffe (fort.):
Newt-slikh-eh Beh-grif-eh:

79. Eine Szene Fehlt
    Eye'neh Stsehn-eh Felt

80. Ans Kopierwerk Schicken
    Ahns Koh-peer-vehrk Shik-en

81. Muss Kodiert Werden
    Mooss Koh-deert Vehr-den

01. Adapter

02. Alternating Current (AC)

03. Aluminum Wire

04. Ambient

05. Ammeter

06. Amperage

07. Ampere

08. Arc Flame

09. Artificial Light

10. Background Light

11. Backlight

12. Bale

13. Ballast

14. Barndoor

Elektrisch
AY-LEK-TRISH

01. Anpassglied
Ahn-pahss-glyte

02. Wechselstrom
Vekh-zel-shtrohm

03. Aluminiumdraht
Ah-loo-min-ee-oom-draht

04. Umfeld
Oom-felt

05. Strommesser
Shtrohm-mess-er

06. Stromstärke
Shtrohm-shtehr-keh

07. Ampere
Ahm-pehr-eh

08. Bogenflamme
Boh-gen-flah-meh

09. Kunstlicht
Koonst-licht

10. Hintergrundlicht/Dekorationslicht
Hin-tehr-groont-likht/Dek-oh-raht-s'yohns-likht

11. Hinterlicht/Gegenlicht
Hin-tehr-likht/Gay-gen-likht

12. Lichtbündel
Likht-bewn-del

13. Ballast
Bah-lahst

14. Lichtblende/Blende/Torblende
Likht-blen-deh/Blen-deh/Tohr-blen-deh

15. Base:

a. bayonet

b. bi-post

c. mogul

d. pin

e. screw

f. threaded

16. Beam

17. Boomlight

18. Bulb:

a. clear

b. frosted

c. gas-filled

d. milky

e. vacuum

16. Sockel/Untergestell:
Zah-kel/Oon-tehr-geh-shtell:

a. Bajonett-
Bah-yoh-net-

b. Doppelfuss-
Dahp-pel-fooss-

c. mogul
moh-gool

d. Nagel
Nah-gel

e. Schraube
Shr'ow-beh

f. gewunden
geh-voon-den

16. Strahl (Träger)
Shtrahl (Treh-ger)

17. Galgen-Licht
Gahl-gen-Likht

18. Birne/Glühlampe
Bihr-neh/Glew-lahm-peh

a. klar
klahr

b. Milchglas
Milkh-glahz

c. gas-gefüllt
gahz-geh-foolt

d. milchig
mihlk-ik

e. vakuum
vahk-oo-oom

19. Buss Bar

20. Cable:

a. single-wire

b. two-wire

c. three-wire

d. ground

e. negative

f. neutral

g. positive

21. Carbon Arc:

a. feed

b. gap

c. crater

d. flame

e. grid

19. Schiene/Verbindungsleiste
Shee-neh/Fehr-bint-oongs-lye-steh

20. Kabel:
Kah-bel:

a. einadrig
eye'n-ah-drik

b. zweiadrig
tsvye-ah-drik

c. dreiadrig
dry-ah-drik

d. Erde
Ayr-deh

e. negativ
nay-gah-teef

f. neutral
noy-trahl

g. positiv
poh-zee-teef

21. Lampenkohle:
Lahm-pen-koh-leh:

a. versorgen
fehr-zohr-gen

b. Spalte
Shpahlt-eh

c. Krater
Krah-ter

d. Flamme
Flahm-meh

e. Netz (Widerstand)
Nehts (Vit-ehr-shtahnt)

21. Carbon Arc (continued):

f. striker

g. sputter

h. hiss

i. underflame

j. white flame

k. yellow flame

22. Carbon Electrode:

a. ionized

b. positive

c. negative

d. copper-jacketed

e. bullet-nosed

23. Circuit Breaker

24. Cluster Lights

21. Lampenkohle (fort.):
Lahm-pen-koh-leh (fawrt.):

f. Zündmechanismus
Tsewnt-may-khahn-ihs-mooss

g. Spratzer
Shpraht-ser

h. zischen
tsis-khen

i. Flammenkern
Flahm-men-kehrn

j. weisse Flamme
vye-seh Flahm-meh

k. gelbe Flamme
gehl-peh Flahm-meh

22. Kohlenelektrode
Koh-len-ay-lek-troh-deh

a. ionisiert
yoh-nih-seert

b. positiv
poh-zih-teef

c. negativ
nay-gah-teef

d. kupfer-überzogen
koop-fehr-ew-behrt-soh-gen

e. kugelkopfförmig
koo-gel-kupf-fuhr-mik

23. Ausschalter/Sicherungsautomat
Owss-shahl-ter/Zikh-eh-roongs-ow-toh-maht

24. Lichtbündel
Likht-boon-del

25. Color Temperature

26. Color Wheel

27. Compact

28. Connector

29. Copper Wire

30. Counter:

    a. hourly

    b. digital

31. Coverage:

    a. beam

    b. field

    c. circular

    d. elliptical

    e. rectangular

25. Farbtemperatur
Farb-tem-pehr-ah-toor

26. Farbenrad
Far-ben-rahd

27. Kompakteil
Kohm-pahk-tile

28. Anschluss
Ahn-shlooss

29. Kupferdraht
Koop-fehr-draht

30. Zähler:
Tsehl-er:

a. stündlich
shtewnd-likh

b. digital
dih-zhih-tahl

31. Reichweite/Versorgung:
Rye-khvye-teh/Fehr-zohr-goong:

a. Scheinwerfer
Shine-vehr-fer

b. Feld
Felt

c. kreisförmig
Krys-fuhr-mig

d. elliptisch
el-lip-tish

e. rechteckig/rechtwinklig
rekh-tek-ik/rekht-vink-likh

32. Connector

a. female-

b. keyed

c. male-

d. pin-

e. stage-

f. straight-blade

g. three-pronged

h. two-pronged

i. twist-lock

33. Current:

a. single-phase

b. three-phase

34. Cut-out Switch

35. Cycle

32. Anschluss:
Ahn-shlooss:

a. Steckdose
Shtek-doh-seh

b. getastet
geh-tah-shtet

c. Stecker
Shtek-er

d. Sperrstift
Shpehr-shtift

e. Stufen-
Shtoo-fen-

f. gerade Klingen
geh-rah-deh Kling-en

g. dreipolig
dry-poh-lig

h. zweipolig
tsvye-poh-lig

i. Drehverschluss
Dreh-fehr-shlooss

33. Strom:
Shtrohm:

a. einphasig
eye'n-fah-zig

b. dreiphasig
dry-fah-zig

34. Pannenschalter/Schutzschalter
Pahn-nen-shahl-tehr/Shoots-shahl-ter

35. Schwingungszug
Shving-oongs-tsoog

36. Dark

37. Dichroic

38. Diffusion

39. Diffusion-holder

40. Dimmer:

 a. magnetic

 b. reactance

 c. resistance

 d. thyristor

41. Dimmer Board

42. Direct Current (DC)

43. Distribution Box

44. Douser

45. Effects Light

46. Electricity

36. Dunkel
Doon-kel

37. Dichroitisch
Dih-kroh-ih-tish

38. Diffusion/Streuung
Dihf-foo-s'yohn/Shtroy-oong

39. Streulichthalter
Shtroy-likht-hahl-ter

40. Lichtregler/Schieber:
Likht-ray-gler/Shee-ber:

a. magnetisch
mahg-nay-tish

b. Blindwiderstand
Blint-vih-dehr-shtahnt

c. Widerstand
Vih-dehr-shtant

d. thyristor
tew-rihs-tor

41. Lichtreglerpult
Likht-ray-gler-poolt

42. Gleichstrom
Gl'eye'kh-shtrohm

43. Abzweigdose/Verteilerkasten
Ahp-tsvyek-doh-zeh/Fehr-tye-ler-kah-sten

44. Feuerschutzklappe
Foy-er-shoot-tsklah-peh

45. Effektlicht
Ehf-fekt-likht

46. Elektrizität
Ay-lek-trits-ih-teht

47. Electrodes

48. Elevate

49. Ellipsoidal

50. Extension Wire

51. Eye-light

52. Feeder Cable

53. Ferrule Contact

54. Field

55. Filament

56. Fill-light

57. Filter

58. Flood

59. Fluorescent

60. Focus Knob

61. Follow-spot

47. Elektroden
Ay-lek-troh-den

48. Heben
Hay-ben

49. Elliptische Linse für kaltes Licht
Ehl-lip-tish Lin-zeh fewr kahl-tes Likht

50. Verlängerungskabel
Fehr-leng-eh-roongs-kah-bel

51. Augenlicht
Ow-gen-likht

52. Antennenkabel
Ahn-ten-nen-kah-bel

53. Ringkontakt
Ring-kohn-tahkt

54. Feld
Felt

55. Glüdraht/Heizfaden
Glew-draht/Hye'ts-fah-den

56. Füllicht/Zusatzlicht/Aufhellicht
Few-likht/Tsoo-zahts-likht/Owf-hell-likht

57. Filter
Fil-ter

58. Fluter/Flutlicht
Floo-ter/Floot-likht

59. Fluoreszent
Floo-oh-rays-tsent

60. Schärferad
Shehr-feh-rahd

61. Verfolgerspot
Fehr-fohl-gehr-shpoht

62. Footcandle

63. Front-light

64. Frosted

65. Fuse

66. Fuse Box

67. Gelatine

68. Generator:

 a. gasoline

 b. diesel

69. Glass:

 a. silica

 b. quartz

70. Grid

71. Head

72. Hertz

62. 10.8 Lux
10.8 Looks

63. Frontallicht/Vorderlicht
Frohn-tahl-likht/Fohr-dehr-likht

64. Mattglas
Maht-glahs

65. Sicherung
Zikh-eh-roong

66. Sicherungskasten
Zikh-eh-roongs-kah-sten

67. Gelatine
Zhel-ah-tee-neh

68. Generator:
Zhen-eh-rah-tohr:

a. Benzin
Bent-seen

b. Diesel
Dee-zel

69. Glas:
Glahs:

a. Silikon
Sih-lih-kohn

b. Quartz
Kvahrts

70. Netz
Nets

71. Leiter
Lye-ter

72. Hertz
Hehrts

73. High

74. High-key

75. HMI:

a. iodides

b. medium-arc

c. mercury

76. Ignition

77. Illumination

78. Incandescent

79. Insulation

80. Intensity

81. Jumper Cable

82. Key-light

83. "Kicker"

84. Kilowatt

73. Hoch
Hohkh

74. Glänzend
Glehnt-sehnt

75. HMI (künstliches Tageslicht)
Hah-Em-Ee (kewnst-likh-ehs Tahk-ehs-likht)

a. Jodid
Yoh-did

b. mittlere Bogenlänge
mit-leh-reh Boh-gen-leng-eh

c. Mercury
Mehr-koo-ree

76. Zündung
Tsewn-doong

77. Beleuchtung
Beh-loykh-toong

78. Glühlampe/Vakuumlampe
Glew-lahm-peh/Vah-koo-oom-lahm-peh

79. Isolierung
Ih-zoh-lee-roong

80. Intensität/Helligkeit
In-ten-sih-teht/Hel-lig-kite

81. Verbindungskabel
Fehr-bin-doongs-kah-bel

82. Hauptlicht/Führungslicht
Howpt-likht/Few-roongs-likht

83. Gegenstreiflicht
Geh-gen-shtrye-flikht

84. Kilowatt
Kil-oh-waht

85. Lamp

86. Lens:

a. clear

b. fresnel

c. plano-convex

d. step-

e. diameter

f. thickness

g. focal point

87. Light:

a. -stand

b. -clamp

c. balance

d. -leak

e. spill-

85. Lampe
Lahm-peh

86. Linse:
Lin-zeh:

a. klar
klahr

b. Stufen-
Shtoo-fen-

c. plankonvex
plahn-kohn-veks

d. Stufen-
Shtoo-fen-

e. Durchmesser
Doorkh-mess-er

f. Dicke
Dik-eh

g. Brennpunkt
Bren-poonkt

87. Licht:
Likht:

a. -stativ
-shtah-tif

b. -klemme
-klem-meh

c. -ausgleich
-owss-glyekh

d. Streuung
Shtroy-oong

e. Streu-/Neben-
Shtroy/Nay-ben-

88. Lighting

89. Load

90. Load Calculation

91. Lock-knob

92. Lock Off

93. Low

94. Low-key

95. Lumen

96. Lumens-per-watt

97. Luminaire

98. Luminaire Ratings:

a. one hundred watt (100w)

b. two hundred watts (200w)

c. two hundred fifty watts (250w)

d. five hundred watts (500w)

88. Beleuchtung
Beh-loyk-toong

89. Belastung
Beh-lahs-toong

90. Belastungsberechnung
Beh-lahs-toongs-beh-rekh-noong

91. Sperrschalter
Shpehr-shahl-ter

92. Festmachen
Fest-mahkh-en

93. Niedrig
Nee-drik

94. Low-key
Low-key

95. Leuchtdichte
Loykht-dikh-teh

96. Leuchdichte pro Watt
Loykht-dikh-teh proh Waht

97. Luminaire
Loo-min-ayr

98. Glühbirnenstärke:
Glew-bihr-nen-shtehr-keh:

a. einhundert Watt (100w)
eye'n-hoon-dehrt Vaht

b. zweihundert Watt (200w)
tsvye-hoon-dehrt Vaht

c. zweihundertfünfzig Watt (250w)
tsvye-hoon-dehrt-fewnf-tsik Vaht

d. fünfhundert Watt (500w)
fewnf-hoon-dehrt Vaht

98. Luminaire Ratings (cont):

    e. five-seventy-five watts (575w)

    f. six hundred watts (600w)

    g. six-fifty watts (650w)

    h. seven-fifty watts (750w)

    i. one thousand watts (1K)

    j. two thousand watts (2K)

    k. twenty-five hundred watts (2500w)

    l. four thousand watts (4K)

    m. five thousand watts (5K)

    n. six thousand watts (6K)

    o. ten thousand watts (10K)

99. Luminous Flux

100. Lug

101. Lux

98. Glühbirnenstärke (fort.):
Glew-bihr-nen-shtehr-keh (fawrt.):

e. fünfhundertundfünfundsiebzig (575w)
fewnf-hoon-dehrt-oont-fewnf-oont-zeep-tsik Vaht

f. sechshundert Watt (600w)
zekhs-hoon-dehrt Vaht

g. sechshundertundfünfzig Watt (650w)
zekhs-hoon-dehrt-oont-fewnf-tsik Vaht

h. siebenhundertundfünfzig Watt (750w)
zee-ben-hoon-dehrt-oont fewnf-tsik Vaht

i. ein tausend (1K)
eye'n t'ow-zent

j. zweitausend (2K)
tsvye-t'ow-zent

k. zweitausendfünfhundert (2500w)
tsvye-t'ow-zent-fewnf-hoon-dehrt

l. viertausend (4K)
feer-t'ow-zent

m. fünftausend (5K)
fewnf-t'ow-zent

n. sechstausend (6K)
zekhs-t'ow-zent

o. zehntausend (10K)
tsehn-t'ow-zent

99. Lichtstrom
Likht-shtrohm

100. Klemme
Kleh-meh

101. Lux
Looks

102. Mains

103. Meter:

   a. am-

   b. ohm-

   c. volt-

104. Mercury Lamp

105. Metal Halide

106. Micro-switch

107. Net

108. Negative

109. Ohm

110. On/Off

111. Paddle

112. Pipe Grid

113. Plastic

102. Netzanschluss/Starkstromnetz
Neht-tsahn-shlooss/Shtahrk-shtrohm-nehtst

103. Messer:
Mess-er:

a. Strom-
Shtrohm-

b. Widerstand-
Vid-er-shtahnt

c. Spannungs-
Shpahn-noongs-

104. Quecksilberlampe
Kvek-zil-ber-lahm-peh

105. Metal Halide
Meh-tahl Hah-lee-deh

106. Mikroschalter
Mik-roh-shahl-ter

107. Softscheibe
Zohft-shy-beh

108. Negativ
Nay-gah-teef

109. Ohm (Widerstand)
Ohm (Vih-der-shtahnt)

110. Ein/Aus
Eye'n/Owss

111. Spatel
Shpah-tel

112. Rohrgitter
Rohr-git-ter

113. Plastik
Plah-steek

114. Plug

115. Plug-in Box

116. Positive

117. Power

118. Power Panel

119. Pre-focus

120. Primary

121. Receptacle

122. Rectifier

123. Reflector:

    a. combination

    b. ellipsoidal

    c. parabolic

    d. round

124. Regulator

114. Kontaktstecker
Kohn-tahkt-shtek-er

115. Steckdose
Shtek-doh-zeh

116. Positiv
Poh-zih-teef

117. Spannung/Leistung
Shpahn-noong/Lye-shtoong

118. Netzschalttafel
Nets-shahll-tah-fel

119. Vorbrennpunkt
Fohr-brehn-poonkt

120. Primärvalenz
Prim-ehr-fah-lents

121. Behälter
Beh-hel-ter

122. Gleichrichter
Glye'kh-rikht-er

123. Aufheller/Hohlspiegel/Reflektor:
Owf-hell-er/Hohl-shpee-gel/Ray-flek-tohr:

a. Kombination
Kohm-bih-naht-s'yohn

b. elliptisch
el-lip-tish

c. Parabol (spiegel)
Pah-rah-bohl (shpee-gel)

d. rund
roont

124. Regler
Ray-gler

125. Rolling Stand

126. Scoop

127. Scrim:

  a. single

  b. double

  c. triple

  d. half-

  e. quarter-

128. Secondary

129. Shadow

130. Short-circuit

131. Shutters

132. Side-light

133. Snoot

134. Socket Adapter

125. Rollstativ
Rohl-shtah-teef

126. Scoop
Skoop

127. Gazeschirm/Softscheibe
Gaht-seh-shirm/Zohft-shye-beh

a. einfach
eye'n-fahkh

b. doppelt
dop-pelt

c. dreifach
dry-fahkh

d. halb
hahlp

e. viertel
feer-tel

128. Sekundär
Zeh-koon-dayr

129. Schatten
Shaht-ten

130. Kurzschluss
Koorts-shlooss

131. Klappeblende
Klahp-peh-blehn-deh

132. Seitenlicht
Zye't-en-likht

133. Scheinwerfernase/Tubus
Shine-fehr-nah-zeh/Too-boos

134. Steckdosenadapter
Shtek-doh-zen-ah-dahp-ter

135. Socket:

  a. single-ended

  b. double-ended

136. Sodium Vapor Lamp

137. Softlite

138. Spill-light

139. Spot

140. Stage Plug

141. Starter

142. Strand (wire)

143. Strip Light (ground row)

144. Sunlight

145. Switch:

  a. single-pole

  b. double-pole

135. Steckdose/Fassung
Shtek-doh-zeh/Fahs-soong

   a. einfache-
   eye'n-fahkh-eh-

   b. Doppel-
   Dop-pel-

136. Natriumdampflampe
Nah-tree-oom-dahmpf-lahm-peh

137. Weiches Licht
Vye-khes Likht

138. Streulicht/Nebenlicht
Shtroy-likht/Nay-ben-likht

139. Spotlicht
Shpaht-likht

140. Bühnen-Stecker
Bew-nen-Shtek-er

141. Anlasser
Ahn-lahs-ser

142. Leitungsdraht
Lye't-oongs-draht

143. Soffittenleuchte
Zohf-fit-ten-loykh-teh

144. Sonnenlicht
Zohn-nen-likht

145. Schalter:
Shahl-ter:

   a. einpolig
   eye'n-poh-lik

   b. zweipolig
   tsvye-poh-lik

146. Template

147. Terminals

148. Tilt:

 a. up

 b. down

149. Top-light

150. Tungsten-halogen

151. Transformer:

 a. step-down

 b. step-up

152. Vent

153. Voltage:

 a. high-

 b. low-

 c. one-hundred-ten

146. Schablone
Shah-bloh-neh

147. Klemmen/Anschlussklemmen
Klehm-men/Ahn-shlooss-klehm-men

148. Gekippt:
Geh-kipt:

a. oben
oh-ben

b. unten
oon-ten

149. Oberlicht
Oh-behr-likht

150. Wolfram-Halogen
Vohl-frahm-Hah-loh-gen

151. Transformator:
Trahnz-fohr-mah-tohr:

a. herunter
hehr-oon-ter

b. herauf
hehr-owf

152. Lüftungsspalt
Lewf-toongs-shpahlt

153. Spannung:
Shpah-noong:

a. hoch
hoh-kh

b. niedrig
nee-drik

c. einhundertundzehn
eye'n-hoon-dehrt-oont-tsehn

153. Voltage (continued):

   d. two-hundred-twenty

   e. three-hundred-eighty

   f. four-hundred-forty

154. Voltage Variation

155. Wire Mesh

156. Yoke

<u>Useful Terms</u>:

157. Danger: High Voltage

158. Do Not Touch

159. Do Not Use Metal Ladder
     In This Vicinity

160. Do Not Use On Electrical Fire

161. Man Working On Line

162. Warning: Not Grounded

153. Spannung (fort.):
Shpahn-noong (fawrt.):

d. zweihundertundzwanzig
tsvye-hoon-dehrt-oont-tsvahn-tsik

e. dreihundertundachtzig
dry-hoon-dehrt-oont-ahkht-tsik

f. vierhundertundvierzig
feer-hoon-dehrt-oont-feer-tsik

154. Spannungsvariation
Shpahn-noongs-vahr-yaht-s'yohn

155. Gitterdraht
Git-ter-draht

156. Joch
Yawkh

Nützliche Begriffe:
Newt-slikh-eh Beh-grif-eh:

157. Gefahr: Hochspannung
Geh-far: Hohkh-shpahn-oong

158. Nicht Berüren!
Nikht Beh-rew-ren!

159. In Diesem Bereich Keine
In Dee-zem Beh-rye'kh Kye-neh

Metalleiter Benutzen!
Meh-tahl-lye-ter Beh-noot-tsen!

160. Keine Heizsonne Benutzen!
Kye-neh Hye'ts-zohn-neh Beh-noot-tsen!

161. Achtung Bauarbeiten!
Ahkh-toong B'ow-ar-bye-ten!

162. Achtung: Nicht Geerdet!
Ahkh-toong: Nikht Geh-ayr-deht!

01. Absorption

02. Achromatic

03. Additive

04. After Image

05. Antihalation

06. Backing

07. Black and White (B&W)

08. Bleach

09. Blow-up

10. Blur

11. Can

12. Characteristic Curve (d log e):

a. shoulder

b. straight line portion of curve

c. toe

01. Absorption
Ahp-zohrp-ts'yohn

02. Achromatisch
Ahkh-roh-mah-tish

03. Additiv
Ahd-dih-teef

04. Nachleuchten (TV)/Nachziehen (film)
Nahkh-loykh-ten/Nahkh-tsee-ehn

05. Lichthofschutz
Likht-hohf-shootst

06. Rückschicht
Rewk-shikht

07. Schwarz und Weiss (S/W)
Shvarts oont Vise (Ess oont Vay)

08. Bleichen
Blye-khen

09. Vergrössern/Blow-up
Fehr-gruss-ehrn/Blow-oop

10. Verwackeln
Fehr-vahk-eln

11. Büchse
Bewkhs-eh

12. Kennlinie Gebiet der
Kehn-lihn-ee Geh-beet dayr

- a. Solarisation in der Schwärzungskurve
  Zoh-lah-rih-zah-ts'yohn ihn dayr Shvehr-tsoongs-koor-veh
- b. gerader Teil einer Kurve
  geh-rahd-er Tile eye'n-er Koor-veh
- c. Fusspunkt
  Fooss-poonkt

13. Cinch Marks

14. Clarity

15. Code Numbers

16. Color:

    a. blue

    b. cyan

    c. green

    d. magenta

    e. red

    f. yellow

    g. white

17. Color Couplers

18. Color Film

19. Color Temperature

20. Composite Daily

13. Kratzer Auf dem Film
    Krah-ter Owf daym Film

14. Klarheit
    Klahr-hyte

15. Kode-Nummern
    Koh-deh-Noom-mehrn

16. Farbe:
    Far-beh:

    a. blau
       bl'ow

    b. blau-grün
       bl'ow-grewn

    c. grün
       grewn

    d. lilarot
       lih-lah-roht

    e. rot
       roht

    f. gelb
       gelp

    g. weiss
       vice

17. Farbmixer
    Farb-mik-ser

18. Farbfilm
    Farb-film

19. Farbtemperatur
    Farb-tem-peh-rah-toor

20. Kombiniertes Muster
    Kohm-bin-eer-tehs Moo-ster

21. Contrast

22. Contrast Range

23. Core

24. Darkroom

25. Daylight Film

26. Defect

27. Deficient

28. Detail

29. Density

30. Densitometer

31. Desaturate

32. Develop:

   a. force one-stop

   b. force two-stops

   c. normal

21. Kontrast
Kohn-trahst

22. Kontrastbereich
Kohn-trahs-beh-ryekh

23. Filmkern/Bobby
Film-kehrn/Boh-bee

24. Dunkelkammer
Doon-kel-kahm-mer

25. Tageslichtfilm
Tahk-eh-shlikht-film

26. Fehler/Schaden
Feh-ler/Shah-den

27. Unzureichend
Oont-soo-rye-khent

28. Detail
Deh-tile

29. Dichte
Dikh-teh

30. Densitometer
Den-zih-toh-may-ter

31. Entsättigen (verweisslichen)
Ent-zeht-tih-gen (fehr-vice-lihkh-en)

32. Entwickeln:
Ent-vik-eln:

a. eine Stufe forcieren
eye'n-eh Shtoo-feh fohr-seer-en

b. zwei Stufen forcieren
tsvye Shtoo-fehn fohr-seer-en

c. normal
nor-mahl

33. Dirt

34. Dye

35. Dupe Negative

36. Edge Number

37. Effluent

38. Emulsion

39. Exposure:

    a. over-exposed

    b. under-exposed

40. Exposure Index

41. Exposure Range

42. Film

43. Filter

44. Fine Grain

45. Fixer

33. Fussel
Foo-sel

34. Farbstoff/Farbe
Farb-shtohf/Far-beh

35. Dupnegativ
Doop-nay-gah-teef

36. Fussnummer
Fooss-noom-mer

37. Abwasser
Ahp-vahs-ser

38. Emulsion/Schicht
Ay-mool-s'yohn/Shikht

39. Belichtung:
Beh-likht-oong:

a. überbelichtet
ew-behr-beh-likht-eht

b. unterbelichtet
oon-tehr-beh-likht-eht

40. Belichtungsindex
Beh-likht-oongz-in-deks

41. Belichtungsspielraum
Beh-likht-oongs-shpeel-r'owm

42. Film
Film

43. Filter
Fil-ter

44. Feinkorn
Fine-kohrn

45. Fixierer
Fiks-eer-er

46. Flash:

a. post-

b. pre-

47. Flat

48. Flesh Tone

49. Fog:

a. edge-

b. full-frame-

50. Frame

51. Frameline

52. Gamma

53. Generation:

a. first

b. second

c. third

46. Blitz
Blihts

a. vor
fohr

b. nach
nahkh

47. Flach
Flahkh

48. Gesichtsfarbe
Geh-zikhts-far-beh

49. Schleier:
Shly-er:

a. Rand-
Rahnt-

b. bildfüllend
bilt-fewl-lent

50. Bildfeld/ Einzelbild
Bilt-felt/Eye'n-tsel-bilt

51. Bildstrich/Bildsteg
Bilt-shtrikh/Bilt-shtek

52. Gamma/Steilheit
Gahm-mah/Shtyle-hyte

53. Generation:
Zheh-neh-raht-s'yohn:

a. erste
ayr-steh

b. zweite
tsvye-teh

c. dritte
drit-teh

54. Grey Scale

55. Grain

56. Granularity

57. High-contrast-positive

58. Highlight

59. Hue

60. Identification Label

61. Infra-red

62. Intermediate

63. Internegative

64. Kelvin Scale

65. Laboratory

66. Latent Image

67. Latitude

68. Light Leak

54. Grau-Skala/Graukeil
Gr'ow-Skah-lah/Gr'ow-kyle

55. Korn
Kohrn

56. Körnigkeit
Kuhr-nik-ite

57. Kontrastreiches Positiv
Kohn-trahst-rye-khes Poh-zih-teef

58. Glanzlicht/Spitzenlicht
Glahnt-slikht/Shpit-sen-likht

59. Farbton
Farb-tohn

60. Aufkleber/Namensschild
Owf-klay-ber/Nah-mens-shilt

61. Infrarot
In-frah-roht

62. Farbzwischenpositiv
Farb-tsvih-shen-poh-zih-teef

63. Internegativ
In-tehr-nay-gah-teef

64. Kelvin-Skala
Kel-vin-Skah-lah

65. Kopierwerk
Koh-peer-vehrk

66. Latentes Bild
Lah-ten-tes Bilt

67. Spielraum
Shpeel-r'owm

68. Lichtenfall
Likht-en-fahl

69. Light Struck

70. Magnetic-striped

71. Motion Picture Film

72. Negative

73. Opaque

74. Original

75. Perforation:

a. double-

b. single-

76. Pitch:

a. long

b. short

77. Print:

a. answer

b. contact

69. Fehlbelichtung/Lichteinfall
Fehl-beh-likht-oong/Likht-eye'n-fahl

70. Mit Magnetrandspur
Mitt Mahg-nay-trahnt-shpoor

71. Spielfilm
Shpeel-film

72. Negativ
Neg-ay-teef

73. Undurchsichtig
Oon-doorkh-zikh-tik

74. Original
Ah-rig-ih-nahl

75. Perforation:
Pehr-foh-raht-s'yohn:

a. doppelseitig
dop-pel-zye-tik

b. einseitig
eye'n-zye-tik

76. Perforationsabstand:
Pehr-foh-raht-s'yohn-zahp-stahnt:

a. lang
lahng

b. kurz
koorts

77. Kopie:
Koh-pee:

a. Erst-/Schnitt-
Ayrst-/Shnitt-

b. Kontakt-
Kohn-tahkt-

77. Print (continued):

c. corrected (timed)

d. one-light

e. optical

f. positive

g. release

78. Print Down

79. Print-scale

80. Print Up

81. Printer-light

82. Rawstock

83. Reciprocity

84. Reduction

85. Resolution

86. Response

77. Kopie (fort.):
Koh-pee (fawrt.):

c. korrigierte
kawr-rig-eer-teh

d. Einlicht-
Eye'n-likht

e. optische-
ohp-tish-eh-

f. positiv
poh-zee-teef

g. Serien-/Vorführ-
Sehr-een-/Fohr-fewr-

78. Verdunkeln
Fehr-doon-keln

79. Kopierverhältnis
Koh-peer-fehr-helt-nihs

80. Verhellen
Fehr-hell-en

81. Kopierlicht
Koh-peer-likht

82. Rohfilmmaterial
Roh-film-mah-tay-r'yahl

83. Resiprozität
Reh-zih-proht-sih-teht

84. Reduktion
Reh-dook-ts'yohn

85. Auflösung
Owf-luss-oong

86. Ansprechen
Ahn-shprekh-en

87. Reversal

88. Rushes

89. Saturation

90. Scratch

91. Sensitivity

92. Shadow

93. Sharpness

94. Silent

95. Silver

96. Solution (liquid)

97. Sound

98. Spool

99. Stain

100. Step-print

101. Still Photograph

87. Umkehr
Oom-kehr

88. Bildmuster
Bilt-moo-ster

89. Sättigung
Set-tik-oong

90. Kratzer/Bildschramme
Kraht-tser/Bilt-shrahm-meh

91. Empfindlichkeit
Emp-fint-likh-kite

92. Schatten
Shah-ten

93. Schärfe
Shehr-feh

94. Stumm
Shtoom

95. Silber
Zil-ber

96. Lösung
Luh-zoong

97. Ton
Tohn

98. Spule
Shpoo-leh

99. Fleck/Einfärbung
Flek/Eye'n-fehr-boong

100. Schrittkopie
Shrit-koh-pee

101. Standfotograf
Shtahnt-foh-toh-grahf

102. Subtractive

103. Test-strip

104. Tone

105. Tungsten Film

106. Ultra-violet

107. Visible Spectrum

108. Wash

109. Water

110. Wavelength

Useful Terms:

111. Keep From Radiation

112. Open In Darkness Only

113. Do Not Expose To Light

114. Darkroom In Use

115. Darkroom: Keep Out

102. Subtraktiv
Zoop-trahk-teef

103. Probestreifen
Proh-beh-shtrye-fen

104. Ton
Tohn

105. Wolfram-Film
Vohl-frahm-Film

106. Ultra-violett
Ool-trah-vih-oh-let

107. Sichtbares Spektrum
Zikht-bah-res Shpek-troom

108. Waschen
Vah-shen

109. Wasser
Vahs-ser

110. Wellenlänge
Vell-en-len-geh

Nützliche Begriffe:
Newt-slikh-eh Beh-grif-eh:

111. Vor Bestrahlung Schützen!
Fohr Beh-shtrah-loong Shewt-tsen!

112. Nur Im Dunkeln Öffnen!
Noor Ihm Doonk-eln Uff-nen!

113. Nicht Licht Aussetzen!
Nikht Likht Ows-zet-tsen!

114. Dunkelkammer In Betrieb!
Doonk-ehl-kahm-mer In Beh-treeb!

115. Dunkelkammer: Eintritt Verboten!
Doonk-ehl-kahm-mer: Eye'n-trit Fehr-boh-ten!

01. Apple Box

02. Backing

03. Bar Clamp

04. Bazooka

05. Black Cloth

06. Blade

07. Breakaway

08. Butterfly

09. Camera Mount

10. Car Mount

11. C-clamp

12. Chain

13. "Cookie"

14. Crane

15. Cukaloris

ATELIERARBEITEN
AH-TEL-YAY-AR-BYE-TEN

01. Kleine Plattform für Schauspieler
Klye-neh Plaht-form fewr Sh'ow-shpee-ler

02. Hintersetzer/Rücksetzer
Hin-ter-zet-tser/Rewk-zet-tser

03. Schraubzwinge
Shr'owb-tsvin-geh

04. Bazooka
Bah-tsoo-kah

05. Schwarzes Tuch
Shvar-tsehs Tookh

06. Blende
Blehn-deh

07. Leichte Atrappen
Lyekh-teh Ah-trah-pen

08. Seidener Schirm
Zye-den-er Shirm

09. Kamerastand
Kah-may-rah-shtahnt

10. Autodachhalterung
Ow-toh-dahkk-hahl-teh-roong

11. C-Klemme
Tsay-Kleh-meh

12. Kette
Ket-teh

13. Schablonen Blende
Shah-bloh-nen Blen-deh

14. Kran
Krahn

15. Schablonen Blende
Shah-boh-nen Blen-deh

16. Cutter

17. Cup Block

18. Cyclorama

19. Diffusion

20. Director's Chair

21. Dolly:

    a. boards

    b. track

    c. curved

    d. section

    e. straight

22. Doorway Dolly

23. Dot

24. Drapery

25. Dulling Spray

16. Grosblende
Grohss-blen-deh

17. Radkeil
Raht-kyle

18. Rundhorizont
Roont-hah-rit-sahnt

19. Streuung/Diffusion
Shtroy-oong/Diff-oo-z'yohn

20. Regiestuhl
Reh-zhee-shtool

21. Kamerawagen
Kah-may-rah-vah-gen

a. Bretter
Breh-ter

b. Schiene
Shee-neh

c. gebogen
geh-boh-gen

d. Teilstrecke
Tyle-shtrek-eh

e. gerade
geh-rah-deh

22. Kleiner Kamerawagen
Klye-ner Kah-may-rah-vah-gen

23. Kleine Rundblende
Klye-neh Roont-blen-deh

24. Vorhänge
For-hen-geh

25. Matt-Spray
Maht-Shpray

26. Elevator

27. Extension-arm

28. Flag

29. Flexible-arm

30. Foil

31. Furniture Pad

32. Grid

33. Grip-clip

34. Grip-kit

35. Grip Stand

36. Gobo

37. Half-apple Box

38. Hanger

39. High-stand

40. Holder

26. Aufzug
Owf-tsook

27. Verlängerungsarm
Fehr-leng-eh-roongs-arm

28. Blende
Blen-deh

29. Schwenkarm
Shvenk-arm

30. Klebeband
Klay-beh-bahnt

31. Möbelschutz
Muh-bel-soots

32. Gitter
Git-ter

33. Klemme
Klehm-meh

34. Werkzeugtasche
Vehrk-tsoyk-tah-sheh

35. Stativ
Shtah-tif

36. Lichtblende
Likht-blen-deh

37. Halbierte Kleine Plattform
Hahl-beert-eh Klye-neh Plaht-form

38. Hänger
Hen-ger

39. Hohe Plattform
Hoh-heh Plaht-form

40. Halter
Hahl-ter

41. Ladder

42. Lockdown Knob

43. Low Stand

44. Meat-axe

45. Metal Frame

46. Net:

    a. open-end

    b. open-side

    c. closed-end

47. Offset-arm

48. Overhead

49. Pancake

50. Parallel

51. Pipe Clamp

52. Pipe Frame

41. Leiter
Lye-ter

42. Verschlusshebel
Fehr-shlooss-hay-bel

43. Niedrige Plattform
Nee-drik-eh Plaht-form

44. Axtform Blende
Ahkst-form Blen-deh

45. Metallrahmen
May-tahl-rah-men

46. Netz:
Nets:

a. offenes Ende
ahf-ehn-es En-deh

b. offene Seite
ahf-en-eh Zite-eh

c. geschlossenes Ende
geh-shlohss-en-es En-deh

47. Ausgleichsarm
Owss-glyekhs-arm

48. Oben Drüber
Oh-ben Drew-ber

49. Dünn Plattform
Dewn Plaht-form

50. Parallel
Pah-rah-lell

51. Rohrklemme
Rohr-kleh-meh

52. Rohrfassung
Rohr-fahss-oong

53. Platform

54. Rails

55. Raincover

56. Reflector:

a. gold

b. hard-side

c. scattered

d. silver

e. soft-side

f. specular

g. stand

h. yoke

i. leaf

57. (to) Rig

58. Rigging

ATELIERARBEITEN (fort.)
AH-TEL-YAY-AR-BYE-TEN (fawrt.)

53. Plattform
Plaht-form

54. Schienen/Geleise
Shee-nen/Geh-lye-zeh

55. Regenschutz
Ray-gen-shoots

56. Reflektor:
Ray-flek-tor:

a. golden
gohl-den

b. harte Seite
hart-eh Zite-eh

c. Streuend
Shtroy-ehnt

d. silber
zil-ber

e. matte Seite
maht-eh Zite-eh

f. Weissspitze
Vice-shpit-tseh

g. Stativ
Shtah-teef

h. Joch
Yawkh

i. Folie
Foh-lee

57. Aufstellen
Owf-shtell-en

58. Auftakelung
Owf-tahk-eh-loong

59. Riser

60. Rope

61. Safety Line

62. Scaffold

63. Scenery

64. Scenic Flat

65. Scrim

66. Shim

67. Show Card

68. Side-arm

69. Silk

70. Skyhook

71. Solid

72. Target

73. Teaser

59. Steigleitung
Shtye-glyet-oong

60. Strick/Seil
Shtrik/Zile

61. Sicherheitslinie
Zikh-er-hyets-lin-ee

62. Gerüst
Geh-rewst

63. Bühnenbild/Dekoration
Bew-nen-bilt/Day-koh-raht-s'yohn

64. Wand
Vahnt

65. Gazeschirm/Softscheibe
Gah-tseh-shirm/Zohft-shy-beh

66. Keil
Kyle

67. Grossen Pappen
Grohs-sen Pahp-pen

68. Seitenarm
Zite-en-arm

69. Seide
Zite-eh

70. Hakenstange
Hah-ken-shtahn-geh

71. Fest
Fehst

72. Gross Rund Blende
Grohss Roont Blen-deh

73. Schwartz Wandschirm
Shvarts Vahnt-shirm

74. Telescopic

75. Trapeze

76. Trombone

77. Tubing

78. Umbrella

79. Wallsled

80. Wedge

81. "Wild"-wall

Useful Terms:

82. Hot Set

83. Keep Clear

84. Keep Off

85. Nail it!

86. Set Brake

87. That's Good!

74. Ausziehbar
Owss-tsee-bar

75. Trapez
Trah-payts

76. Posaune
Poh-z'ow-neh

77. Schlauch/Rohr
Shl'owkh/Rohr

78. Schirm
Shirm

79. Wandhalterung für Lichtquelle
Vahnt-hahlt-er-oong fewr Likht-kvell-eh

80. Besenkeil
Beh-zen-kyle

81. Bewegliche Wand
Beh-vek-likh-eh Vahnt

Nützliche Begriffe:
Newt-slikh-eh Beh-grif-eh:

82. Achtung Dreharbeiten!
Ahk-toong Dray-ar-bye-ten!

83. Fernbleiben
Fehrn-blye-ben

84. Eintritt Verboten
Eye'n-tritt Fehr-boh-ten

85. Das Ist Es!
Dahss Isst Ess!

86. Drehpause
Dray-p'ow-zeh

87. Das Ist Gut!
Dahss Isst Goot!

Useful Terms (continued):

88. Watch Your Head

89. Wear a Hardhat

90. Wear Protective Glasses

91. Just a little more!

92. Too Much!

93. Just a Little Less

94. To the Left

95. To the Right

Nützliche Begriffe (fort.):
Newt-slikh-eh Beh-grif-eh (fawrt.):

88. Achtung! Geringe Höhe
Ahkh-toong! Geh-rin-geh Huh-heh

89. Bitte Schutzhelm
Bit-eh Shoots-helm

90. Bitte Schutzbrille Tragen!
Bit-eh Shoots-brill-eh Trah-gen!

91. Ein Bisschen Mehr!
Eye'n Bihs-shen Mehr!

92. Zu Viel!
Tsoo Feel!

93. Ein Bisschen Weniger!
Eye'n Bihs-shen Vehn-ih-ger

94. Mehr Links!
Mehr Links!

95. Mehr Rechts!
Mehr Rekhts!

01. Ambience

02. Amplifier

03. Amplitude Modulation (AM)

04. Attenuation

05. Audio

06. Automatic-level-control

07. Background Noise

08. Baffle

09. Balance

10. Bass

11. Batteries

12. Boom (equipment)

13. Boom (hollow sound)

14. Bridge

15. Bulk Eraser

TON
TOHN:

01. Raumkulisse
R'owm-koo-liss-eh

02. Verstärker
Fehr-shtehr-ker

03. Amplitudenmodulation (AM)
Ahm-plee-too-den-moh-doo-laht-s'yohn (Ah-Em)

04. Abschwächung/Dämpfung
Ahp-shvekh-oong/Dempf-oong

05. Niederfrequenz (NF)
Nee-der-fray-kvents (En-Ef)

06. Automatische Pegelaussteuerung
Ow-toh-mah-tish-eh Pay-gel-owss-shtoy-eh-roong

07. Hintergrund Ton
Hin-tehr-groont Tohn

08. Schallwand/Absorbierende Wand
Shahl-vahnt/Ahp-zohr-beer-end-eh Vahnt

09. Ausgleich
Owss-glyekh

10. Tiefton
Teef-tohn

11. Batterien
Baht-teh-reen

12. Galgen
Gahl-gen

13. Dröhnen
Druh-nen

14. Brücke
Brewkh-eh

15. Löschgerät
Lush-geh-reht

16. Cable

17. Capstan

18. Cassette

19. Change Tape

20. Channel

21. Circuit

22. Cleaner

23. Commentary

24. Composite

25. Connector

26. Console

27. Contacts

28. Cross-cut

29. Cross-fade

30. Cue

16. Kabel
Kah-bel

17. Bandtransportrolle
Bahnt-trahnz-pohrt-rohl-leh

18. Kassette
Kahs-set-teh

19. Bandwechsel
Bahnt-vekh-zel

20. Kanal
Kah-nahl

21. Stromkreis
Shtrohm-kryez

22. Reiniger
Rye-nih-ger

23. Kommentar/Sprechertext
Kohm-men-tahr/Shprekh-er-tekst

24. Kombinierte Bild-Tonkopie
Kohm-bin-eer-teh Bilt-Tohn-koh-pee

25. Anschluss/Verbindung
Ahn-shlooss/Fehr-bin-doong

26. Konsole
Kohn-zohl-eh

27. Kontakte
Kohn-tahk-teh

28. Montage
Mon-tahzh

29. Mischen Einblendung
Mis-shen Eye'n-blen-doong

30. Zeichen
Tsye-khen

31. Crystal Control

32. Decibel

33. Degauss

34. Dialogue

35. Distortion

36. Double System

37. Dual Track

38. Dub

39. Dubbing

40. Dupe

41. Effects

42. Electronics

43. Equalize

44. Extension

45. Fade-in

31. Quarzsteuerung
Kvarts-shtoy-roong

32. Dezibel
Dayt-see-bel

33. Entmagnetisieren
Ent-mahg-net-ee-see-ren

34. Dialog
Dih-ah-lohg

35. Verzerrung
Fehrt-sehr-roong

36. Doppelsystem
Dop-pel-zew-staym

37. Zweispur/Doppelspur
Tsvye-shpoor/Dop-pel-shpoor

38. Kopieren/Anlegen
Koh-peer-en/Ahn-lay-gen

39. Kopieren
Koh-peer-en

40. Duppen/Duplikat
Doop-pen/Doop-lih-kaht

41. Effekte
Ef-fek-teh

42. Elektronik
Ay-lek-troh-neek

43. Ausgleichen
Owss-glye-khen

44. Verlängerung
Fehr-leng-eh-roong

45. Einblendung
Eye'n-blen-doong

46. Fade-out

47. Fidelity

48. Final Mix

49. Fishpole (hand-held boom)

50. Flutter

51. Frequency:

 a. high-

 b. low-

52. Frequency Modulation (FM)

53. Frequency Response

54. Generator

55. Headphones

56. Hum

57. Inches-per-second

58. Input

46. Ausblende
Owss-blen-deh

47. Tonqualität
Tohn-kvahl-ih-tet

48. Endmischung
Ent-mish-oong

49. Kleiner Handgalgen
Klye-ner Hahnt-gahl-gen

50. Flackern
Flahk-ern

51. Frequenz:
Fray-kvents:

a. Hoch-
Hoh-kh-

b. Nieder-
Nee-der-

. equenzmodulation (FM)
ray-kvents-moh-doo-laht-s'yohn (Ef-Em)

53. requenzgang
Fray-kvents-gahng

54. Generator
Gen-eh-rah-tohr

55. Kopfhörer
Kupf-huh-rer

56. Brummton
Broom-tohn

57. Bandgeschwindigkeit
Bahnt-geh-shvin-dik-kite

58. Eingang
Eye'n-gahng

59. Interlock

60. Interview

61. Iron-oxide

62. Jack

63. Laydown

64. Lead-in

65. Lip-sync

66. (to) Loop

67. Looping

68. Loud

69. Lower Register

70. Maintenance

71. Magnetic Stock:

a. fullcoat

b. striped

59. Interlock
In-tehr-lock

60. Interview
In-tehr-v'yew

61. Eisenoxyd
Eye-zen-ahk-zewd

62. Buchse
Bookh-zeh

63. Bestimmen
Beh-shtim-men

64. Einfürung/Einleitung
Eye'n-few-roong/Eye'n-lye-toong

65. Lippensynchron
Lip-pen-zew-khrohn

66. Schleifen
Shlye-fen

67. Schleifeneinrichtung
Shlye-fen-eye'n-rikh-toong

68. Laut
L'owt

69. Tiefen
Tee-fen

70. Wartung
Vahr-toong

71. Magnettonmaterial:
Mahg-net-tohn-mah-tay-r'yahl:

a. Magnetband
Mahg-net-bahnt

b. Magnetspur
Mahg-net-shpoor

72. Magnetic Transfer

73. Master

74. Microphone:

a. bidirectional

b. directional

c. condenser

d. hand

e. lapel

f. lavalier

g. non-directional

h. omni-directional

i. shotgun

j. uni-directional

k. wireless

75. Microphone Lines

72. Überspielung auf Magnetton
Ew-ber-shpee-loong owf Mahg-net-tohn

73. Original
Oh-rih-gih-nahl

74. Mikrofon:
Mik-roh-fohn:

a. zweiseitiges Richt-
tsvye-zite-ik-es Rikht-

b. gerichtetes-
geh-rikh-teh-tes

c. Kondensator-
Kohn-den-sah-tohr-

d. Hand-
Hahnt-

e. Ansteck-/Knopfloch-
Ahn-shtek-/K'nahpf-flokh-

f. Lavallier
Lah-vahl-leer

g. ungerichtetes
oon-geh-rikh-teh-tes

h. richtungsunempfinliches/Kugel
rikh-toongs-oon-emp-fin-likh-es/Koo-gel

i. Richt-
Rikht-

j. einseitig gerichtetes/Richt-
eye'n-zite-ik geh-rikh-teh-tes/Rikht

k. drahtloses
draht-lohs-es

75. Mikrofondrähte
Mihk-roh-fohn-dreht-eh

76. Mid-range

77. Mix

78. Mix-down

79. Mix Panel

80. Modulated:

 a. over-

 b. under-

81. Monaural

82. Multiple Track

83. Music

84. Musical Score

85. Narration

86. Noise:

 a. high-

 b. low-

76. Mittlere Reichweite
Mitt-lehr-eh Ryekh-vite-eh

77. Mischung
Mih-shoong

78. Ausblenden
Owss-blen-den

79. Mischpult
Mish-poolt

80. Moduliert/Ausgesteuert:
Moh-doo-leert/Owss-geh-shtoy-ehrt:

a. übersteuert
ew-ber-shtoy-ehrt

b. untersteuert
oon-ter-shtoy-ehrt

81. Einohrig
Eye'n-oh-rik

82. Mehrspurig
Mehr-spoo-rik

83. Musik
Moo-zeek

84. Partitur der musik
Pahr-tih-toor dehr Moo-zeek

85. Sprechertext/Begleitext
Shprekh-er-tekst/Beh-glite-ekst

86. Lautstärke:
L'ow-shtehr-keh

a. hoch
hoh-kh

b. niedrig
nee-drik

87. Optical:

 a. stock

 b. track

 c. transfer

88. Oscillator

89. Out-of-sync

90. Ouput

91. Peak

92. Pick-up

93. Pin

94. Playback Head

95. Plug

96. Post-production Mix

97. Post-synchronize

98. Potentiometer

87. Optisch:
Ohp-tish

a. Material
Mahtay-r'yahl

b. Spur
Shpoor

c. überspielen
ew-ber-shpee-len

88. Oszillator
Ohs-tsih-lah-tor

89. Asynchron
Ah-sewn-krohn

90. Ausgabe
Owss-gah-beh

91. Spitze/Scheitel
Shpit-tseh/Shye-tel

92. Tonabnehmer
Tohn-ahp-neh-mer

93. Sperrstift
Shpehr-shtift

94. Wiedergabekopf
Vee-der-gah-beh-kupf

95. Stecker/Steckkontakt
Shtek-er/Shtek-kohn-tahkt

96. Mischung Nach der Produktion
Mih-shoong Nakh dehr Proh-dookt-s'yohn

97. Nachsynchronisation
Nakh-sewn-kroh-nee-zaht-s'yohn

98. Potentiometer
Poh-tent-s'yoh-may-ter

99. Power Consumption

100. Pre-amplifier

101. Public Address System

102. Quality

103. Range

104. Receiver

105. Receptacle

106. Record (noun)

107. Record (adj)

108. Recorded Tape

109. Recording Channel

110. Recording Head

111. Reel

112. Reel-to-reel

113. Re-record

99. Stromaufnahme
Shtrohm-owf-nah-meh

100. Vorverstärker
For-fehr-shter-ker

101. Lautsprecheranlange
L'owt-shprek-er-ahn-lahn-geh

102. Qualität
Kvahl-ih-tet

103. Reichweite
Ryekh-vite-eh

104. Empfänger
Emp-fen-ger

105. Behälter
Beh-hel-ter

106. Schallplatte
Shahl-plah-teh

107. Ton Aufnahmen
Tohn Owf-nah-men

108. Bespieltes Tonband
Beh-shpeel-tes Tohn-bahnt

109. Aufnahmekanal
Owf-mah-meh-kahl

110. Aufnahmekopf
Owf-nah-meh-kupf

111. Spule
Shpoo-leh

112. Umspulen
Oom-shpoo-len

113. Überspielen
Ew-behr-shpeel-en

114. Resolver

115. Re-wind

116. Room Tone

117. Rustle

118. Rhythmic

119. Scene

120. Scratch Track

121. Shielded Wire

122. Sibilants

123. Single-track

124. Single-system

125. Smooth

126. Soft

127 Solid State

114. Löschkopf
Lush-kupf

115. Zurückspulen
Tsew-rewk-shpoo-len

116. Raumton
R'owm-tohn

117. Rascheln
Rah-sheln

118. Rhytmisch
Rit-mish

119. Szene
Stseh-neh

120. Arbeitston
Ar-bites-tohn

121. Abgeschirmter Draht
Ahp-geh-shirm-ter Draht

122. Zischlaut
Tsish-l'owt

123. Einspur
Eye'n-shpoor

124. Eisnspursystem
Eye'n-shpoor-sew-staym

125. Weich
V'eye'kh

126. Sanft/Leise
Sahnft/Lye'zeh

127. Transistoriert
Trahn-zis-tawr-eert

128. Sound:

a. -edit

b. -effect

c. -head

d. -proof

e. -library

f. -recording

g. report

h. tape

129. Sound-on-film

130. Speaker

131. Splice:

a. bevel

b. straight

c. taped

128. Ton:
Tohn:

a. -schnitt
-shnitt

b. -effekt
-eff-ekt

c. -kopf
-kupf

d. Schalldicht
Shahl-dikht

e. -archiv
-arkh-eef

f. -aufnahme
-owf-nah-meh

g. -bericht
-beh-rikht

h. -band
-bahnt

129. Filmton
Film-tohn

130. Sprecher
Shprekh-er

131. Kleben:
Klay-ben:

a. Schrägkante
Shrek-kahn-teh

b. gerade
geh-rah-deh

c. geklebt
geh-klept

132. Static

133. Stereophonic

134. Switch

135. Sync

136. Synchronous

137. Sync Mark

138. Sync Pops

139. Sync Pulse

140. Take

141. Talk-back

142. Tape Recorder

143. Toggle-switch

144. Tone

145. Track

146. Transcribe

132. Statisch
Shtah-tish

133. Stereophon
Stay-ray-oh-fohn

134. Schalter
Shahl-ter

135. Synchron
Zewn-khrohn

136. Synchron
Zewn-khrohn

137. Synchronmarke
Zewn-khrohn-mahr-keh

138. Synchronimpuls Akustisch
Zewn-khrohn-im-poolss Ah-koo-tish

139. Synchronimpuls
Zewn-khrohn-im-poolss

140. Aufnahme/Take
Owf-nah-meh/Take

141. Gegensprechanlage
Geh-gen-shprekh-ahn-lah-geh

142. Tonbandgerät
Tohn-bahnt-geh-ret

143. Kippschalter
Kipp-shahl-ter

144. Ton
Tohn

145. Spur
Shpoor

146. Überspielen
Ew-ber-shpee-len

147. Transfer

148. Transistor

149. Tube

150. Turntable

151. Treble

152. Upper Register

153. Virgin Tape

154. Voice Level

155. VU (Volume Units) Meter

156. Meter

157. Wow

Useful Terms:

158. Composite Track (voice, music, effects)

159. Dialogue Track

160. Do Not Magnetize

147. Überspielen
Ew-ber-shpee-len

148. Transistor
Trahn-zis-tawr

149. Röhre
Ruh-reh

150. Plattonteller
Plaht-tohn-tell-er

151. Hochton
Hohkh-tohn

152. Höhen
Huh-hen

153. Leerband
Layr-bahnt

154. Stimmhöhe
Shtim-huh-heh

155. VU-Meter
Vay-Oo-May-ter

156. Messgerät
Mess-geh-reht

157. Jauler/Heuler
Y'ow-ler/Hoy-ler

Nützliche Begriffe:
Newt-slikh-eh Beh-grif-eh:

158. Gemischte Spur (Stimme, Musik, Geräusche)
Geh-mish-teh Shpoor (Shtim-eh, Moo-zeek, Geh-roy-sheh)

159. Dialog-Band
Dih-ah-lohk-Bahnt

160. Nicht Magnetisieren
Nikht Mahg-net-tihs-eer-en

Useful Terms (continued):

161. Effects Track

162. Master

163. Music and Effects Combined

164. Music Track

165. To Be Transfered

166. Voice Track

Nützliche Begriffe (fort.):
Newt-slikh-eh Beh-grif-eh (fawrt.):

161. Geräuschbänder
Geh-roysh-bent-er

162. Mutterband
Moo-tehr-bahnt

163. Gemischtes Musikband und Geräuschband
Geh-mish-tehs Moo-zeek-bahnt oont Geh-roysh-bahnt

164. Musikband
Moo-zeek-bahnt

165. Zu Überspielen
Tsoo Ew-ber-shpeel-en

166. Sprachband
Shprahkh-bahnt

01. Above The Line

02. Accounting

03. Advertising

04. Agent

05. Agreement

06. Audit

07. Authority

08. Below The Line

09. Bookkeeping

10. Budget:

a. final

b. over-

c. preliminary

d. under-

e within

PROH-DOOKT-S'YOHN-BEW-ROH

01. Im Budget
Eem Bood-zhet

02. Buchhaltung
Bookh-hahl-toong

03. Werbung
Vehr-boong

04. Agent
Ah-zhent

05. Vertrag
Fehr-trahk

06. Buchprüfung
Bookh-prew-foong

07. Behörde
Beh-huhr-deh

08. Unterm Strich
Oon-tehrm Shtrikh

09. Buchhaltung
Bookh-hahl-toong

10. Budget:
Bood-zhet:

a. endgültiges
ent-gewl-tih gehs

b. über
ew-ber

c. vorläufiges
for-loy-fih-gehs

d. unter
oon-ter

e. im
eem

11. Business

12. Buyout

13. Clearance

14. Completion Bond

15. Confirmation

16. Contract

17. Corporate Overhead Expense

18. Corporation

19. Department Head

20. Disbursements

21. Distribution

22. Employ

23. Employer

24. Entertainment

25. Executive

11. Geschäft
    Geh-sheft

12. Überbieten
    Ew-ber-bee-ten

13. Ausverkauf/Ausräumung
    Owss-fehr-k'owf/Owss-roy-moong

14. Bürgschaft
    Bewrg-shahft

15. Bestätigung
    Beh-steht-ih-goong

16. Vertrag
    Fehr-trahk

17. Handlungsunkosten
    Hahnt-loongs-oon-koh-sten

18. Gesellschaft
    Geh-zell-shahft

19. Abteilungsleiter
    Ahp-tile-oongs-lye-ter

20. Auszahlung
    Owss-tsah-loong

21. Verteilung
    Fehr-tile-oong

22. Einstellen
    Eye'n-shtell-en

23. Arbeitgeber
    Ar-bite-geh-ber

24. Unterhaltung
    Oon-ter-hahlt-oong

25. Geschäftsführer
    Geh-shefts-few-rer

26. Exhibition

27. Fee

28. Finance

29. Financing

30. General Office Overhead

31. Incorporate

32. Independent Contractor

33. Insurance:

   a. life

   b. public liability

   c. disability

   d. worker's compensation

   e. accident

34. Joint Venture

35. Investor

26. Ausstellung
Owss-shtell-oong

27. Honorar
Hoh-nah-rahr

28. Finanzen
Fih-nahn-tsen

29. Finanzierung
Fin-nahn-tseer-oong

30. Bürokosten
Bew-roh-koh-sten

31. Gesellschaft
Geh-zell-shahft

32. Unabhängiger Auftragnehmer
Oon-ahp-hen-gih-ger Owf-trahk-nay-mer

33. Versicherung:
Fehr-zikh-er-oong:

a. Lebens-
Lay-benz-

b. Haftpflicht-
Hahft-pflikht-

c. Ausfall-
Owss-fahll-

d. Arbeitsausgleich-
Ar-bite-s'ows-glyekh-

e. Unfall-
Oon-fahl-

34. Gemeinsames Unternehman
Geh-mine-zah-mehs Oon-tehr-nay-mahn

35. Kapitalanleger
Kah-pih-tahl-ahn-lay-ger

36. Lease

37. Legal Counsel

38. Legal Fees

39. License

40. Limited Partners

41. Location Scouting

42. Management

43. Miscellaneous

44. Money

45. Negotiation

46. Office

47. Officer:

   a. President

   b. Executive Vice-President

   c. Vice-President

36. Mietvertrag
Meet-fehr-trahk

37. Rechtsberatung
Rekhts-beh-rah-toong

38. Rechtsanwaltskosten
Rekhts-ahn-vahlts-koh-sten

39. Lizenz
Lit-sents

40. Beschränkte Partnerschaft
Beh-shrenk-teh Pahrt-nehr-shahft

41. Drehortsuche
Dray-hort-zookh-eh

42. Management/Führung/Leitung
Mah-nahzh-ment/Few-roong/Lye-toong

43. Verschiedenes
Fehr-shee-deh-nes

44. Geld
Gelt

45. Verhandlung
Fehr-hahnt-loong

46. Büro
Bew-roh

47. Vorstandmitglieder/Funktionäre:
Fohr-shtahnt-mit-glee-der/Foonkt-s'yohn-ehr-eh:

a. Präsident
Preh-zih-dent

b. Geschäftsführender Vizepräsident
Geh-shefts-few-ren-der Veet-seh-preh-zih-dent

c. Vizepräsident
Veet-seh-preh-zih-dent

47. Officer (continued)

d. Treasurer

e. Secretary

f. Chairperson

g. Chairperson of the Board

h. Chief Executive Officer

48. Outside Expenses

49. Partnership

50. Pension Contributions

51. Permission

52. Permit

53. Phone and Telegraph

54. Policy

55. Preview

47. Vorstandmitglieder/Funtionäre (fort.):
Fohr-shtahnt-mit-glee-der/Foonkt-s'yohn-ehr-eh (fawrt.):

d. Schatzmeister/Kassenverwalter
Shahts-mye-ster/Kah-sen-fehr-vahl-ter

e. Sekretär/Sekretärin
Zek-reh-tehr/Zek-reh-tehr-in

f. Vorsitzender
Fohr-zit-tsen-der

g. Aufsichtsratsvorsitzender
Owf-zikhts-rahts-for-zit-tsend-er

h. Geschäftsführendes Vorstandsmitglied
Geh-shefts-few-rent-es For-shtahnts-mit-gleet

48. Sonstige Unkosten
Zoh-shtik-eh Oon-koh-sten

49. Partnerschaft
Pahrt-nehr-shahft

50. Sozialversicherung
Zoh-ts'yahl-fehr-zikh-er-goong

51. Erlaubnis/Gehnehmigung
Ehr-l'owp-nis/Geh-nay-mik-oong

52. Erlaubnis
Ehr-l'owp-nis

53. Telefon und Telegraf
Teh-leh-fohn oont Teh-leh-grahf

54. Politik
Poh-lih-teek

55. Vorabaufführung
Fohr-ahb'owf-few-roong

56. Production:

a. pre-

b. post-

c. staff

57. Proprietor

58. Publicity

59. Purchases

60. Release

61. Rent and Utilities

62. Rentals

63. Rules

64. Salaries

65. Schedule

66. Staff

67. Star

56. Produktion:
Proh-dookt-s'yohn:

   a. Vor-
   For-

   b. Nach-
   Nahkh-

   c. -stab
   -shtahp

57. Inhaber
In-hahb-er

58. Werbung
Vehr-boong

59. Einkauf
Eye'n-k'owf

60. Verleih
Fehr-lye

61. Miete und Unkosten
Meet-eh oont Oon-koh-sten

62. Leihgeräte
Lye-geh-reht-eh

63. Vorschriften/Regeln
Fohr-shrif-ten/Ray-geln

64. Gehälter
Geh-helt-er

65. Programm/Zeitplan
Proh-grahm/Tsite-plahn

66. Personal
Pehr-zoh-nahl

67. Hauptdarsteller
H'owpt-dar-shtell-er

68. Studio

69. Supplies and Postage

70. Taxes:

a. business

b. city

c. corporate

d. county

e. federal

f. municipal

g. state

71. Travel Expense:

a. airplane/automobile

b. ship/train

c. economy

d. first class

68. Studio
Shtoo-d'yoh

69. Büromaterial und Postgebühren
Bew-roh-mah-tay-r'yehl oont Pohst-geh-bew-ren

70. Steuern:
Shtoy-ern:

a. Gewerbe-
Geh-vehr-beh-

b. Gemeinde-
Gehm-eye'n-deh-

c. Umsatz-
Oom-zahtst-

d. Landkreis
Lahnt-kryz

e. Bundes
Boon-des

f. Städtisch
Shteht-tish

g. Staat
Shtaht

71. Reisekosten:
Rye-zeh-koh-sten:

a. Flugzeug/Auto
Flook-tsoyk/Ow-toh

b. Schiff/Eisenban
Shiff/Eye-zen-bahn

c. zweite Klasse
tsvye-teh Klahs-seh

d. erste Klasse
ayr-steh Klahs-seh

Useful Terms:

72. Accounts Payable/Receivable

73. Charge To:

74. Credit/Debit

75. Hold In Suspense

76. Memo To:

77. Paid In Full

78. Verified

<u>Nützliche Begriffe</u>:
Newt-slikh-eh Beh-grif-eh:

72. Konto für Einzahlungen/Auszahlungen
Kohn-toh fewr Eye'n-tsah-loon-gen/Owss-tsah-loon-gen

73. Rechnung an:
Rekh-noong ahn:

74. Soll/Haben
Zohl/Hah-ben

75. In der Schwebe Halten
In dehr Shveh-beh Hahl-ten

76. Aktennotiz an:
Ahk-ten-noh-teets ahn:

77. Vollständig Bezahlt
Fohl-shtehn-dik Beh-tsahlt

78. Geprüft
Geh-prewft

01. Action

02. Add

03. Aside

04. Asterisk

05. Atmosphere

06. Audio

07. Away

08. Background (b.g.)

09. Caption

10. Character

11. Close (shut)

12. Continued

13. Cut

14. Dash (—)

15. Day

DREHBUCH-BEGRIFFE

DRAY-BOOKH-BEH-GRIF-FEH

01. Achtung Aufnahme/Action
Akh-toong Owf-nah-meh/Ahk-ts'yohn

02. Hinzufügen
Hin-tsoo-few-gen

03. Beiseite
Bye-zite

04. Sternchen
Shtehrn-khen

05. Stimmung
Shtim-moong

06. Ton
Tohn

07. Fort/Weg
Fort/Vek

08. Hintergrund
Hin-ter-groont

09. Überschrift/Text zu Einem Bild
Ew-ber-shrift/Tekst tsoo Eye'n-em Bilt

10. Besetzung
Beh-zet-tsoong

11. Zumachen
Tsoo-mahkh-en

12. Weitermachen
Vye-ter-mahkh-en

13. Schneiden
Shnye-den

14. Bindestrich
Bint-eh-shtrikh

15. Tag
Tahk

16. Delete

17. Dialect

18. Dialogue

19. Dissolve

20. Down

21. Downstage

22. Effect

23. Enter

24. Eraser

25. Exclamation Point

26. Exit

27. Exterior

28. Fade-in

29. Fade-out

30. Footnote

16. Weglassen/Auslassen
Veh-glahs-sen/Ows-lah-sen

17. Dialekt
Dih-ah-lekt

18. Dialog
Dih-ah-lohk

19. Auflösen
Owf-luh-sen

20. Hinunter
Hin-oon-ter

21. Im Vorderen Teil der Bühne
Im Fohr-dehr-en Tile dehr Bew-neh

22. Effekt
Eff-ekt

23. Fintritt
Fin-tritt

24. Radiergummi
Rah-deer-goom-mee

25. Ausrufezeichen
Owss-roof-eh-tsye-khen

26. Ausgang
Owss-gahng

27. Aussen
Owss-en

28. Aufblende
Owf-blehn-deh

29. Abblende
Ahp-blehn-deh

30. Fussnote
Fooss-noh-teh

31. From

32. Glossary

33. Hyphen

34. Indent

35. Index

36. In Frame

37. Ink

38. Intercut

39. Interior

40. Interpret

41. Language

42. Left

43. Left-to-right

44. Mood

45. More

31. Von
Fahn

32. Zusammenfassung
Tsoo-zahm-men-fahs-soong

33. Bindestrich
Bint-eh-shtrikh

34. Finrückung
Fin-rewk-oong

35. Inhaltsverzeichniss
In-hahlts-fehr-tsyekh-niss

36. Bildframe
Bilt-frah-meh

37. Tinte
Tin-teh

38. Zwischenschnitt
Tsvih-shen-shnitt

39. Innen
Ih-nen

40. Darstellen
Dahr-shtell-en

41. Sprache
Shprah-khe

42. Links
Links

43. Von Links Nach Rechts
Fahn Links Nahkh Rekhts

44. Stimmung/Laune
Shtim-moong/L'ow-neh

45. Mehr
Mehr

46. Narration

47. Night

48. Notation

49. Off-screen (o.s.)

50. Open

51. Out-of-frame

52. Page

53. Pen

54. Pencil

55. Period (.)

56. Picture

57. Plot

58. Point Of View (P.O.V.)

59. Question Mark

60. Quote

46. Erzählung
Ehr-tseh-loong

47. Nacht
Nahkht

48. Notiz
Noh-teets

49. Off
Ahf

50. Offen
Ahf-fen

51. Nicht Im Bildfeld
Nikht Im Bilt-felt

52. Seite/Blatt
Zye-teh/Blaht

53. Füllfeder/Kugelschreiber
Fewl-fay-der/Koo-gel-shrye-ber

54. Bleistift
Blye-shtift

55. Punkt
Poonkt

56. Bild
Bilt

57. Handlung
Hahnt-loong

58. Standpunkt
Shtahnt-poonkt

59. Fragezeichen
Frah-geh-tsye-khen

60. Zitieren
Tsit-eer-ren

61. Re-write

62. Right

63. Right-to-left

64. Ruler (measuring)

65. Scenario

66. Scene

67. Screenplay

68. Script

69. Sequence

70. Shooting Script

71. Shot

72. Sound

73. Stage Left

74. Stage Right

75. Story

61. Überarbeitung
Ew-ber-ar-bite-oong

62. Rechts
Rekhts

63. Von Rechts Nach Links
Fahn Rekhts Nahkh Links

64. Lineal
Lih-neh-ahl

65. Szenarium
Stsay-nahr-ih-oom

66. Szene
Stsay-neh

67. Drehbuch
Dray-bookh

68. Drehbuch
Dray-bookh

69. Sequenz
Zay-kvents

70. Drehbuch
Dray-bookh

71. Aufnahme
Owf-nah-meh

72. Ton
Tohn

73. Linke Bühnenseite
Lin-keh Bew-nen-zyte-eh

74. Rechte Bühnenseite
Rekh-teh Bew-nen-zyte-eh

75. Geschichte
Geh-shikh-teh

76. Synopsis

77. Sub-plot

78. Superimpose

79. The End

80. Theme

81. Title

82. To

83. Toward

84. Treatment

85. Type

86. Typewriter

87. Typewriter Ribbon

88. Write

89. Video

76. Synopse
Tsew-nohp-zeh

77. Nebenhandlung
Nay-ben-hahnt-loong

78. Überblenden
Ew-ber-blen-den

79. Das Ende
Dahss End-eh

80. Thema
Tay-mah

81. Titel
Tee-tel

82. Zu
Tsoo

83. Gegen/Auf/Zu
Gay-gen/Owf/Tsoo

84. Treatment
Tray-aht-ment

85. Maschinenschreiben
Mah-sheen-en-shrye-ben

86. Schreibmaschine
Shryeb-mah-sheen-eh

87. Schreibmaschinenband
Shryeb-mah-sheen-en-bahnt

88. Schreiben
Shrye-ben

89. Video
Vih-deh-oh

Useful Terms:

90. First Draft

91. Final

92. Revised

93. Approved

94. Registered

95. Copyright

96. Original Script

97. O.K. To Duplicate

98. Send To Printer

Nützliche Begriffe:
Newt-slikh-eh Beh-grif-eh:

90. Erster Entwurf
Ayr-ster Ent-voorf

91. Endfassung
End-fahs-soong

92. Überarbeitat
Ew-ber-ar-bite-aht

93. Akzeptiert
Ahk-tsep-teert

94. Protokolliert
Proh-toh-kohl-leert

95. Copyright
Koh-ee-rite

96. Original Skript
Ah-rig-ih-nahl

97. Kopierbereit
Koh-peer-beh-rite

98. Zur Druckerei Schicken
Tsoor Drook-eh-rye Shik-en

01. Awl

02. Belt

03. Blade

04. Block-and-tackle

05. Blowtorch

06. Bolt

07. Broom

08. Brush:

a. artist's

b. camel's-hair

c. paint

d. wire

e. narrow

f. wide

09. Bull-horn

WERKZEUG
VEHRK-TSOYK

01. Ahle
Ah-leh

02. Gürtel
Gewr-tel

03. Klinge
Kling-eh

04. Flaschenzug
Flah-shen-tsook

05. Schneidbrenner
Shnyed-brehn-er

06. Bolzen/Riegel
Bohl-tsen/Ree-gel

07. Besen
Bay-zen

08. Pinsel:
Pin-zel:

a. eines Künstlers
eye'n-es Kewnst-lers

b. Kamelhaar-
Kah-mel-hahr-

c. Mal-
Mahl-

d. Drahtbürste
Draht-bewr-steh

e. schmaler
shmahl-er

f. breiter
brye'ter

09. Megaphon
Meh-gah-fone

10. Caliper

11. C-clamp

12. Chisel:

    a. metal

    b. narrow-blade

    c. wide-blade

    d. wood

13. Compass

14. Countersink

15. Dividers

16. Drill:

    a. concrete

    b. metal-cutting

    c. "star"

    d. wood-cutting

10. Taster
Tah-ster

11. Schraubklemme
Shr'owp-kleh-meh

12. Meissel:
Mye-sell:

a. Metall-
Meh-tahl-

b. schmaler
shmahl-er

c. breiter-
brye-ter

d. Holz-
Hohlts-

13. Zirkel
Tsir-kehl

14. Versenker/Spitzsenker
Fehr-zen-ker/Shpits-tsenker

15. Teiler/Stechzirkel
Tye'ler/Shtek-tsir-kel

16. Bohrer:
Boh-rer:

a. Beton-
Beh-tohn-

b. Metall-
Meh-tahl-

c. Betonmeissel
Beh-tohn-mye-sehl

d. Holz
Hohlts

17. English Scale

18. File:

a. bastard

b. half-round

c. mill

d. pointed

e. round

f. tapered

19. Flaring Tool

20. Flashlight

21. Fuse Puller

22. Gloves

23. Hammer:

a. ball pein

b. claw

17. Englischer Mass-stab
Eng-lish-er Mahss-shtahp

18. Feile:
Fye-leh:

a. flache-
flah-sheh-

b. halbrunde-
hahl-broon-deh-

c. Holz-
Hohlts-

d. spitze-
shpit-tseh-

e. runde-
roon-deh-

f. spitze zulaufende
shpit-tseh tsoo-l'owf-end-eh

19. Streckenwerkzeug
Shtreh-ken-wehrk-tsoyk

20. Taschenlampe
Tah-shen-lahm-peh

21. Sicherungszieher
Zikh-eh-roongs-tsye-er

22. Handschuhe
Hahnt-shoo-eh

23. Hammer:
Hahm-mer

a. Rundkopf-
Roont-kupf-

b. Tischler-
Tish-ler-

23. Hammer (continued):

c. machinest's

d. rawhide

e. rubber

f. scaling

g. sledge

h. tack

i. upholsterer's

24. Handle

25. Hoe

26. Hoist

27. Hook

28. Jack:

a. hydraulic

b. screw

23. Hammer (fort.):
Hahm-mer (fawrt.):

c. Maschinisten-
Mah-shin-ih-sten-

d. Leder-
Lay-der-

e. Gummi-
Goom-mee-

f. Schale
Shah-leh

g. Vorschlag-
Fohr-shlahk-

h. leichter
lyekh-ter

i. Tapezierers
Tahp-eh-tseer-ers

24. Griff
Griff

25. Hacke
Hah-keh

26. Aufzug/Kran
Owf-tsook/Krahn

27. Haken/Klammer
Hah-ken/Klahm-mer

28. Wagenheber:
Vah-gen-hay-ber:

a. hydraulischer-
hew-dr'ow-lish-er

b. schraubbarer
shr'owb-bahr-er

29. Kit

30. Knife:

a. carpet

b. electrician's

c. hunting

d. pocket

e. putty

f. razor-blade

31. Lubricant:

a. grease

b. grease-gun

c. oil

d. oil can

e. oil spout

f. rustproof

29. Werkzeugkiste
Vehrk-tsoyk-kis-teh

30. Messer:
Mess-er:

a. Teppich-
Tep-pish-

b. Elektrikers-
Ay-lek-trik-ers-

c. Jagd-
Yahkt-

d. Taschen-
Tah-shen-

e. Kitt-
Kitt-

f. Rasier-
Rah-zeer-

31. Schmiermittel
Shmeer-mit-tel

a. Fett/Schmiere
Feht/Shmeer-eh

b. Ölpistole
Uhl-pih-stoh-leh

c. Öl
Uhl

d. Ölkanne
Uhl-kahn-neh

e. Ölausfluss Schnabel
Uhl-ows-flooss Schnah-bel

f. Rostsicher
Rohst-zikh-er

32. Magnifying Glass

33. Measuring Tape:

a. carpenter's

b. cloth

c. folding

d. metal

e. pocket

f. ruler

34. Metric Scale

35. Nail

36. Needle:

a. hypodermic

b. sailmaker's

c. sewing

d. tailor's

32. Magnifierglas
Mahg-nih-feer-glahz

33. Massband:
Mahss-bahnt:

a. Schreiners-
Shrye-ners

b. Tuch-
Tookh-

c. Mass-stab
Mahss-shtahp

d. Metall-
Meh-tahl-

e. Taschen-
Tah-shen-

f. Lineal
Lin-eh-ahl

34. Metrische Skala
May-trish Skah-lah

35. Nagel
Nah-gel

36. Nadel:
Nah-del:

a. Injektions-
In-yek-ts'yohns-

b. Segelmachers-
Zay-gel-mahkh-ers-

c. Näh-
Neh-

d. Näh-
Neh-

37. Nut

38. Pick

39. Pitchfork

40. Pliers:

a. battery

b. diagonals

c. fence

d. ignition

e. insulated-handle

f. knurled-handled

g. lineman's

h. needle-nose

i. serrated-jaw

j. side-cutting

k. slip-joint

37. Schraubenmutter
Shr'ow-ben-moot-er

38. Pickel
Pik-el

39. Heugabel
Hoy-gah-bel

40. Zangen:
Tsahn-gen:

a. Batterie-
Baht-teh-ree-

b. diagonal-
dih-ah-goh-nahl

c. Draht-
Draht-

d. isolierte-
ih-zoh-leer-teh

e. isolierte- tem Griff
ih-zoh-leer-teh- tehm Grif

f. mit geriffel- tem Griff
mitt geh-rif-fel- tehm Grif

g. Elektrikers-
Ay-lek-trik-ers-

h. Rund-Spitz-
Roont-Shpits-

i. Kombinations-
Kohm-bin-aht-s'yohns-

j. Seitenschneider
Zye-ten-shnye-der

k. verstellbar
fehr-shtell-bar

40. Pliers (continued):

l. smooth-jaw

m. snap-ring

n. water pump

o. wire-cutting

41. Pouch

42. Pry Bar

43. Punch

44. Rake

45. Rivet

46. Rivet Gun

47. Safety Goggles

48. Saw:

a. back-

b. electrical-powered

40. Zangen (fort.):
Tsahn-gen (fawrt.):

l. Flach-
Flahkh-

m. Schnappring-
Shanhp-ring-

n. Wasserpumps
Vahs-ser-poompz

o. Drahtschneider
Draht-shnye-der

41. Tasche
Tah-sheh

42. Brechstange
Brekh-shtahn-geh

43. Locher
Lokh-er

44. Rechen
Rehkh-en

45. Nieten
Nee-ten

46. Nietmaschine
Neet-mah-sheen-eh

47. Schutzbrille
Shoots-bril-leh

48. Säge:
Zeh-geh:

a. steifgrat-
shtife-graht-

b. elektrische-
ay-lek-trish-eh-

48. Saw (continued):

c. hack-

d. hand-

e. keyhole

f. metal

g. tree-

49. Scraper

50. Screw

51. Screwdriver:

a. insulated

b. jeweler's

c. large

d. medium

e. offset

f. Phillips

48. Säge (fort.):
Zeh-geh (fawrt.):

c. Metall-
May-tahl-

d. Hand-
Hahnt-

e. Laub-
L'owp-

f. Metall-
May-tahl-

g. Baum-
B'owm-

49. Schaber
Shah-ber

50. Schraube
Shr'ow-beh

51. Schraubenzieher:
Shr'ow-ben-tsee-er:

a. isulierter-
ih-zoo-leer-ter-

b. kleiner-
klyne-er

c. grosser-
groh-ser-

d. mittelgrosser-
mit-el-groh-ser-

e. versetzter-
fehr-zet-tster-

f. Phillips
Fill-ips

51. Screwdriver (continued):

g. plastic

h. small

i. straight-blade

j.. technician's

52. Shank

53. Sheave

54. Shovel

55. Solder

56. Soldering Iron

57. Spade

58. Sponge

59. Swivel

60. Stopwatch

51. Schraubenzieher:
Shr'ow-ben-tsee-er:

g. Plastik-
Plah-steek-

h. kleiner-
klye-ner-

i. geradeblatt
geh-rah-deh-blaht

j. technikers-
tekh-nik-ers-

52. Stiel
Shteel

53. Schaft
Shahft

54. Schaufel
Sh'ow-fel

55. Lötdraht
Luht-draht

56. Löteisen
Luht-eye-zen

57. Spaten
Shpah-ten

58. Schwamm
Shvahm

59. Drehgelenk
Dray-gel-enk

60. Stoppuhr
Shtohp-poor

61. Tape:

a. black

b. camera

c. cloth

d. double-face

e. electrician's

f. gaffer's

g. masking

h. paper

62. Tin Snips

63. Tool Box

64. Trowel:

a. brick

b. jointer

c. linoleum

61. Klebeband:
Klay-beh-bahnt:

a. schwarzes-
shvar-tsehs-

b. Kamera-
Kah-may-rah-

c. Lassoband
Lahs-soh-bahnt

d. doppelseitiges
dop-pel-zite-ih-ges

e. Isolierband
Ih-zoh-leer-bahnt

f. grauband
gr'ow-bahnt

g. Klebeband
Klay-beh-bahnt

h. Klebeband
Klay-beh-bahnt

62. Metallschere
Meh-tahl-shehr-eh

63. Werkzeugkiste
Vehrk-tsoyk-kis-teh

64. Kelle:
Kehl-leh:

a. Mauerer-
M'ow-er-er

b. Glätteisen
Gleht-eye-zehn

c. Linoleum-
Lih-noh-lay-oom

64. Trowel (continued):

d. planting

e. plastering

f. pointing

65. Tube Cutter

66. Welding Torch

67. Winch

68. Wire Stripper

69. Work Light

70. Wrench:

a. adjustable

b. close-ended

c. combination

d. mechanic's

e. open-ended

64. Kelle (fort.):
Kehl-leh (fawrt.):

d. Kleine Gartenschaufel
Klye-neh Gahr-ten-sh'ow-fel

e. Stukkateur-
Shtook-kah-tewr-

f. spitze-
shpit-seh-

65. Rohrschneider
Rohr-shnye-der

66. Schweissbrenner
Shvyess-breh-ner

67. Seilwinde
Zyle-vint-eh

68. Ab-isolierzange
Ahp-iz-oh-leer-tsahn-geh

69. Arbeitslicht
Ar-bite-slikht

70. Schraubenschlüssel
Shr'ow-ben-shlew-sel

a. verstellbar
fehr-shtell-bar

b. Ringschlüssel
Ring-shlew-sell

c. Kombinationssatz
Kohm-bih-naht-s'yohns-zahts

d. Mechanikers
Mehkh-ahn-ih-kers

e. Maulschlüssel
M'ow-shlew-sel

70. Wrench (continued):

f. plumber's

g. ratchet

h. socket

i. torque

Useful Terms:

71. Keep Out

72. Keep Off

73. Wet Paint

74. Hard Hat Required

75. Wear Safety Glasses

76. Unsafe

77. First Aid Kit

78. Fire Extinguisher

79. In An Emergency Call....

70. Schraubenschlüssel
Shr'ow-ben-shlew-sel

f. Rohrzange
Rohr-tsahn-geh

g. kleine Rohrzange
kline-eh Rohr-tsahn-geh

h. Steckschlüssel
Shtek-shlew-sel

i. Drehmoment
Dray-moh-ment

<u>Nützliche Begriffe</u>:
Newt-slkih-eh Beh-grif-eh:

71. Eintritt Verboten!
Eye'n-trit Fehr-boh-ten!

72. Eintritt Verboten!
Eye'n-trit Fehr-boh-ten!

73. Frisch Gestrichen!
Frish Geh-shtrikh-en!

74. Schutzhelm Erforderlich!
Shoot-ts-helm Ehr-fawr-der-likh!

75. Schutzbrille Muss Getragen Werden!
Shoot-ts-bril-leh Mooss Geh-trah-gen Vehr-den!

76. Nicht Abgesichert!
Nikht Ahp-geh-zikh-ert!

77. Erste Hilfe Kasten
Ayr-steh Hil-feh Kah-sten

78. Feuerlöscher
Foy-er-luh-sher

79. Im Falle Eines Notfalls Bitte...Anrufen
Im Fah-leh Eye-nes Noht-fahls Bit-teh ... Ahn-roo-fen

01. Adjust

02. Ambience

03. Amplifier

04. Amplify

05. Amplitude

06. Anode

07. Antenna

08. Apparatus

09. Aspect Ratio

10. Audio

11. Automatic Gain Control

12. Beam-splitter

13. Bias

14. Black Level

15. Blanking

VIDEO
VIH-DAY-OH

01. Einstellen/Justieren/Richten
Eye'n-shtell-en/Yoo-steer-en/Rikh-ten

02. Raumkulisse
R'owm-koo-lihs-seh

03. Verstärker
Fehr-shtehr-ker

04. Verstärken
Fehr-shtehr-ken

05. Amplitude
Ahm-plih-tood-eh

06. Anode
Ah-nohd-eh

07. Antenne
Ahn-ten-neh

08. Apperat/Gerät
Ahp-peh-raht/Geh-reht

09. Bildformat
Bilt-fawr-maht

10. Niederfrequenz
Nee-der-fray-kvents

11. Automatische Verstärkungsregelung
Ow-toh-mah-tish-eh/Fehr-shtehrk-oongs-ray-geh-loong

12. Strahlenhalter
Shtrah-len-hahl-ter

13. Gitterspannung
Git-ter-shpahn-noong

14. Schwarzwert/Schwarzpegel
Shvarts-vehrt/Shvarts-pay-gel

15. Austaten/Schwarztastung
Ow-shtaht-en/Shvarts-tahst-oong

16, Blanking Pulse

17. Bloom

18. Booster

19. Brightness

20. Calibrate

21. Cathode

22. Camera Chain

23. Channel

24. Chroma

25. Chroma-key

26. Chrominance

27. Circuit

28. Clip (cut-off)

29. Closed Circuit

30. Co-axial Cable

16. Vertikalaustastimpuls
Fehr-tik-ahl-owss-tahst-im-pools

17. Überstrahlung
Ew-ber-shtrah-loong

18. Booster/Verstärker
Boo-ster/Fehr-shtehr-ker

19. Helligkeit
Hell-ik-kite

20. Eichen/Kalibrieren
Eye-khen/Kah-lib-ree-ren

21. Kathode
Kah-tohd-eh

22. Kamera-Kette
Kah-may-rah-Ket-teh

23. Kanal
Kah-nahl

24. Farb-
Farb-

25. Farbschablonentrick
Farb-shah-bloh-nen-trik

26. Chrominanz
Kroh-min-ahnts

27. Stromkreis
Shtrohm-kryez

28. Abschneiden
Ahp-shnye-den

29. Kurzschlussverfahren
Koorts-shlooss-fehr-fah-ren

30. Koaxialkabel
Koh-ahk-s'yahl-kah-bel

31. Color:

 a. -balance

 b. -bars

 c. -killer

 d. temperature

32. Commercial

33. Compatible

34. Compositor

35. Confetti

36. Console

37. Contrast

38. Contrast Range

39. Control

40. Control Room

41. Convergence

31. Farb:
Farb:

a. -abstimmung
-ahp-shtim-moong

b. -balken
-bahl-ken

c. -abschaltung/-sperre
-ahp-shahl-toong/-shpehr-eh

d. -temperatur
-tem-peh-rah-toor

32. Kommerziell
Kohm-mehr-tsih-ell

33. Kompatibel
Kohm-pah-tih-bel

34. Schriftsetzgerät
Shrift-zet-tsgeh-reht

35. Konfetti
Kohn-fet-tee

36. Konsole
Kohn-zoh-leh

37. Kontrast
Kohn-trahst

38. Kontrastbereich
Kohn-trahst-beh-ryekh

39. Schaltung/Steuerung
Shal-toong/Shtoy-er-oong

40. Kontrollraum/Regieraum
Kohn-trohl-r'owm/Reh-zhee-r'owm

41. Konvergenz
Kohn-fehr-gents

42. Copy

43. Cue

44. Current

45. Damping

46. DC Restorer

47. Definition

48. Deflecting Yoke

49. Detector

50. Diode

51. Distortion

52. Drop Frame

53. Duplicate

54. Duplicator

55. Edit

56 Electron Beam

42. Kopie
Koh-pee

43. Zeichen/Markierung
Tsye-khen/Mahrk-eer-oong

44. Strom
Shtrohm

45. Dämpfung
Demp-foong

46. Schwarzwertwiedergeber
Shvarts-vehrt-vee-der-geh-ber

47. Kantenschäfe/Schärfe
Kahn-ten-shef-eh/Shehrf-eh

48. Ablenkvorrichtung
Ahp-lenk-fohr-rikh-toong

49. Detektor
Day-tek-tohr

50. Diode
Dih-oh-deh

51. Verzerrung
Fehr-tsehr-roong

52. Beweglicher Rahmen
Beh-vek-likh-er Rah-men

53. Duplikat
Doop-lih-kaht

54. Duplikator
Doop-lih-kaht-ohr

55. Schneiden/Montieren
Shnye-den/Mohn-teer-en

56. Elektronenstrahl
Ay-lek-troh-nen-shtrahl

57. Electron Gun

58. Electronic Camera

59. Exposure:

a. over-

b. under-

60. Field

61. Film-to-tape

62. Fine Tuning

63. Fringing

64. Gain

65. Gamma

66. Ghost

67. Grey Card

68. Grey Scale

69. Grid-leak

57. Elektronen Kanone
Ay-lek-trohn-en Kah-nohn-eh

58. Elektronische Kamera
Ay-lek-troh-nish-eh Kah-may-rah

59. Belichtung:
Beh-likh-toong:

a. über-
ew-ber-

b. unter-
oon-ter-

60. Feld
Felt

61. Film auf Band
Film owf Bahnt

62. Scharfabstimmung
Sharf-ahp-shtim-moong

63. Unschärfe/Farbverlust
Oon-shehrf/Farb-fehr-loost

64. Verstärkung
Fehr-shtehr-koong

65. Gamma/Steilheit
Gah-mah/Shtyle-hite

66. Geisterbild
Gye-ster-bilt

67. Graukarte
Gr'ow-kahr-teh

68. Grauskala
Gr'ow-skah-lah

69. Gitterwiderstand
Git-ter-vit-er-shtahnt

70. Headphones

71. High Band

72. Hold:

a. horizontal

b. vertical

73. Hue

74. Hum

75. Image

76. Image Plate

77. Impedence

78. In-frame Coding

79. Interference

80. Interlace

81. Joy-stick

82. Keystone

70. Kopfhörer
Kupf-huh-rer

71. Hochband
Hohkh-bahnt

72. Standbild:
Shtahnt-bilt:

   a. Zeilenfangregler
   Tsye-len-fahng-ray-gler

   b. Bildfangregler
   Bilt-fahng-ray-gler

73. Farbton
Farb-tohn

74. Brumm
Broom

75. Bild
Bilt

76. Bildplatte
Bilt-plaht-teh

77. Impedanz
Im-pay-dahnts

78. Biltfelt Numerieren
Bihlt-fehlt Noo-mehr-ee-rehn

79. Interferenz/Störung
In-tehr-fehr-ents/Shtuh-roong

80. Zwischenspannung
Tsvih-shen-shpahn-noong

81. Fernbedienung
Fehrn-beh-dee-noong

82. Trapezverzerrung
Trah-pets-fehr-tsehr-roong

83. Kinescope

84. Knob

85. Line

86. Linear

87. Light-and-shade

88. Limiter

89. Luminance

90. Master

91. Matrix

92. Micro:

a. -switch

b. -volt

93. Modulation:

a. over-

b. under-

83. Fernsehröhre
Fehrn-zeh-ruh-reh

84. Knopf
K'nahpf

85. Zeile
Tsye-leh

86. Linear
Lin-eh-ahr

87. Licht und Schatten
Likht oont Shaht-ten

88. Begrenzer
Beh-gren-tser

89. Luminanz
Loo-min-ahnts

90. Original
Oh-rig-ih-nahl

91. Matrix
Mah-treeks

92. Mikro:
Mih-kroh:

a. -schalter
-shahl-ter

b. -stromstärke
-shtrohm-shtehr-keh

93. Modulation:
Moh-doo-lah-ts'yohn:

a. übermodilierung
ew-ber-moh-dih-leer-oong

b. untermodilierung
oon-ter-moh-dih-leer-oong

94. Monitor

95. Multi-camera

96. Negative Image

97. Noise:

a. low-

b. high-

c. off-line

98. Oscilloscope

99. Peak

100. Pedestal

101. Phosphor

102. Photoconductor

103. Photoelectric Cell

104. Picture Tube

105. Pincushion Effect

94. Monitor
Moh-nih-tohr

95. Mehrere Kameras
Mehr-eh-reh Kah-may-rahs

96. Negativbild
Nay-gah-teef-bilt

97. Geräusch:
Geh-roysh:

a. rauscharm
r'ow-sharm

b. lautes-
l'ow-tehs-

c. off-line
awf-lin-eh

98. Oszillograf
Ohs-tsil-loh-grahf

99. Scheitel
Shye-tel

100. Schwarzabhebung
Shvarts-ahp-hay-boong

101. Leuchtphosphor
Loykht-foh-sfor

102. Fotoleiter
Foh-toh-lye-ter

103. Fotoelektrische Zelle
Foh-toh-ay-lek-trish-eh Tsel-eh

104. Fernsehröhre
Fehrn-zeh-ruh-reh

105. Kissenverzerrung
Kiss-en-fehr-tsehr-roong

106. Pipe Grid

107. Positive

108. Power Supply

109. Printed Circuit

110. Program

111. Pulse Shaper

112. Radiation

113. Range

114. Receiver

115. Raster

116. Red-Green-Blue (RGB)

117. Reflectance

118. Remote

119. Satellite

120. Saturation

106. Rohrgitter
Rohr-git-ter

107. Positiv
Poh-zih-teef

108. Netzanschluss
Net-tsahn-shlooss

109. Gedruckter Schaltkreis
Geh-drook-ter Shahlt-kryes

110. Programm
Proh-grahm

111. Impulsformer
Im-pools-fawr-mer

112. Ausstrahlung
Owss-shtrahl-oong

113. Bereich/Reichweite
Beh-ryekh/Ryekh-vite-eh

114. Empfänger
Ehmp-fehn-ger

115. Bildraster
Bilt-rah-ster

116. Rot-Grün-Blau (RGB)
Roht-Grewn-Bl'ow (Er-Gay-Bay)

117. Remission
Reh-miss-yohn

118. Fernsteuerung
Fehrn-shtoy-er-roong

119. Satellit
Zah-tell-it

120. Sättigung
Zet-tih-goong

121. Sawtooth Waveform

122. Scanner

123. Secondary Emission

124. Selector Switch

125. Semi-conductor

126. Shunt

127. Signal

128. Signal-to-noise Ratio

129. Sine Wave

130. Slo-mo Disc

131. Snow

132. Straight Frame

133. Synchronizer

134. Switcher (vision mixer panel)

135. Sync Generator

121. Sägezahnfömige Welle
Zeg-eh-tsahn-fuh-mih-geh Vel-leh

122. Abtaster
Ahp-tahs-ter

123. Zweit-Strahlung
Tsvyet-Shtrah-loong

124. Wahlschalter
Vahl-shahl-ter

125. Halbleiter
Hahl-blye-ter

126. Nebenschluss
Nay-ben-shlooss

127. Signal/Zeichen
Zig-nahl/Tsye-khen

128. Geräuschunterschied Zwischen Modiliertem
Geh-roysh-oonter-sheet Tsvih-shen Moh-dih-leer-tem

129. Sinuswelle
Zin-oos-vell-eh

130. Zeitlupenscheibe
Tsite-loop-en-shye-beh

131. Schnee
Shnay

132. Gerade Biltfelt
Geh-rah-deh Bihlt-fehlt

133. Synchronisator
Zewn-kroh-nih-zah-tor

134. Schaltpult
Shahlt-poolt

135. Synchrongenerator
Zewn-kroh-nih-zah-tor

136. Tape-to-film

137. Television

138. Test Pattern

139. Title:

  a. crawl

  b. roll

  c. still

  d. sub-

140. Tonal Proportion

141. Tone

142. Transfer

143. Transistor

144. Transmission

145. Translator

146. Transmitter

136. Band auf Film
Bahnt owf Film

137. Fernsehen
Fehrn-zay-en

138. Testbild
Test-bilt

139. Titel:
Tee-tel:

a. langsam Roll
lahng-sahm Rohl

b. Roll
Rohl

c. Standbild
Shtahnt-bilt

d. unter
oon-tehr

140. Grau-Verhältnis
Gr'ow-Fehr-helt-nis

141. Ton
Tohn

142. Überspielung
Ew-ber-shpeel-oong

143. Transistor
Trahn-zis-tor

144. Sendung/Übertragung
Zen-doong/Ew-ber-trahg-oong

145. Umsetzer
Oom-zet-tser

146. Sender
Zen-der

147. Trichromatic Colors

148. Tuner

149. Tube

150. UHF (ultra-high-frequency)

151. VHF (very-high-frequency)

152. Voltage:

    a. high

    b. low

153. Volume

154. Waveform Monitor

155. White Card

Useful Terms:

156. Standby

157. On Air

158. Off Air

147. Dreifarbenverfahren
Dry-fahr-ben-fehr-fahr-en

148. Tuner
Too-ner

149. Röhre
Ruh-reh

150. UHF (Ultra Hohe Frequenz)
Oo-Hah-Ef (Ool-trah Hoh-eh Fray-kvents)

151. VHF (Sehr Hohe Frequenz)
Fow-Hah-Ef (Zehr Hoh-eh Fray-kvents)

152. Spannung:
Shpahn-noong:

a. Hoch-
Hohkh-

b. niedrige
nee-drih-geh

153. Volumen
Voh-loo-men

154. Wellenform Monitor
Vel-len-fawrm Moh-nih-tohr

155. Weiss Karte
Vice Kahr-teh

Nützliche Begriffe:
Newt-slikh-eh Beh-grif-eh:

156. Bereitschaft
Beh-rite-shahft

157. Sendung
Zen-doong

158. Sendeschluss
Zen-deh-shlooss

01. Allowance

02. Apprentice

03. Artist

04. Benefits:

a. fringe

b. health and welfare

c. holiday

d. pension

e. retirement

f. vacation

05. Bonus

06. Business Agent

07. Call:

a. cancellation of

b. change of

ARBEITSAUSDRÜCKE
AR-BITES-OWSS-DREW-KHEH

01. Taschengeld
Tah-shen-gelt

02. Anzulernender
Ahn-tsool-ehr-nen-der

03. Künstler
Kewnst-ler

04. Soziale Leistungen:
Zaht-s'yahl Lye-stoong-en:

a. züsätzliche Leistungen
tsoo-zet-tslikh-eh Lye-stoong-en

b. Kranken und Sozialhilfe
Kyahn-ken oont Zaht-s'yahl-hil-feh

c. Feiertage
Fye-er-tahk-eh

d. Pension/Altersrente
Pon-s'yohn/Ahl-tehrz-ren-teh

e. Pensionierung
Pon-s'yohn-eer-oong

f. Urlaub
Oor-l'owp

05. Bonus
Bahn-oos

06. Verbindung Agent
Fehr-bin-doong Ah-gent

07. Anruf:
Ahn-roof:

a. Absage von
Ahp-zah-geh fahn

b. Veränderung von
Fehr-ent-er-oong fahn

07. Call (continued):

c. day-

d. maximum

e. night-

f. minimum

08. Callback

09. Check

10. Classification:

a. higher

b. lower

11. Conditions

12. Consecutive

13. Craft

14. Crew

15. Crew Member

07. Anruf (fort.):
Ahn-roof (fawrt.):

c. Tages
Tahk-ehs

d. maximal
mahks-ih-mahl

e. Nacht
Nahkht

f. minimal
min-ih-mahl

08. Zurück rufen
Tsoo-rewk roo-fen

09. Überprüfen
Ew-ber-prew-fen

10. Einteilung:
Eye'n-tile-oongç

a. höher
huh-er

b. niedriger
nee-drig-er

11. Bedingungen
Beh-ding-oon-gen

12. Fortlaufend
Fawrt-l'owf-ent

13. Kunsthandwerk
Koonst-hahnt-vehrk

14. Arbeitsteam
Ar-bites-teh-ahm

15. Mitarbeiter
Mit-ar-bite-er

16. Cumulative

17. Day Work

18. Deductions

19. Dependent

20. Dismiss

21. Dismissal Time

22. Dismiss For Cause

23. Employee:

a. daily

b. female

c. hourly

d. male

e. weekly

f. staff

24. Employer

16. Gesamt/Häufung
Geh-zahmt/Hoy-foong

17. Die Arbeit Eines Tages
Dee Ar-bite Eye'nes Tahk-es

18. Abzüge
Ahp-tsew-geh

19. Angehörige/Abhängige
Ahn-geh-huh-rih-geh/Ahp-heng-ih-geh

20. Entlassen
Ent-lahs-sen

21. Entlassungstermin
Ent-lahs-soongs-tehr-min

22. Entlassungsgrund
Ent-lahs-soongs-groont

23. Angestellter:/Angestellte:
Ahn-geh-shtel-ter:/Ahn-geh-shtel-teh:

a. täglich
tahk-likh

b. weiblich
vye-blikh

c. stündlich
shtewnt-likh

d. männlich
men-likh

e. wöchenlich
vuh-khen-likh

f. Mitarbeiterstab
Mit-ar-bite-er-shtahp

24. Arbeitsgeber
Ar-bites-geh-ber

25. Employment

26. Experienced

27. Expenses

28. First Unit

29. Freelance

30. Foreman

31. Forelady

32. Grievance

33. Guild

34. Hazard Pay

35. Hire

36. Independent Contractor

37. Insurance

38. Layoff

25. Anstellung
Ahn-shtel-loong

26. mit Erfahrung
mit Ehr-fah-roong

27. Ausgaben/Kosten
Owss-gah-ben/Koh-sten

28. Erste Schicht
Ayr-steh Shikht

29. Freiberuflich
Frye-beh-roof-likh

30. Vorarbeiter
Fawr-ar-bite-er

31. Vorarbeiterin
Fawr-ar-bite-er-in

32. Beschwerde
Besh-vehrt-eh

33. Zunft/Gilde/Verein
Tsoonft/Gil-deh/Fehr-eye'n

34. Gefahren Geld
Geh-fah-ren Gelt

35. Anstellen
Ahn-stellen

36. Selbstständiger Auftragnehmer
Zelpst-shten-dih-ger Owf-trahk-neh-mer

37. Versicherung
Fehr-zikh-er-oong

38. Entlassungen
Ent-lahs-soong-en

39. Location:

a. distant

b. nearby

40. Lodgings

41. Meal Penalty

42. Meal Period

43. Night Premium

44. Non-union

45. On Call

46. Overnight

47. Pay:

a. -day

b. -off

c. -master

d. -rate

39. Drehort:
Dray-ort:

a. weit weg
vite vehg

b. in der Nähe
in dehr neh-eh

40. Unterkunft
Oon-ter-koonft

41. Extra Bezahlung für Nicht Essen
Eks-trah Beh-tsah-loong fewr Nikht Ehss-ehn

42. Essenzeit
Ess-en-tsyet

43. Nachtzuschlag
Nahkht-tsoo-shlahk

44. Nicht der Gewerkschaft Angehörig
Nikht dehr Geh-vehrk-shahft Ahn-geh-huh-rik

45. Auf Abruf
Owf Ah-broof

46. Über Nacht
Ew-ber Nahkht

47. Bezahlung:
Beh-tsah-loong:

a. Tagesspesen
Tahk-ess-shpay-zen

b. Abzahlung
Ahp-tsah-loong

c. Zahlmeister
Tsahl-mye-ster

d. Tagessatz
Tahk-es-zahts

48. Per Diem

49. Person

50. Personnel

51. Premium Pay

52. Promotion

53. Quitting Time

54. Rate:

    a. basic hourly

    b. daily

    c. weekly

55. Re-run

56. Residual

57. Rest Period

58. Second Unit

59. Severance

48. Pro Tag
Proh Tahk

49. Person
Pehr-zohn

50. Mitarbeiterstand
Mit-ar-bite-er-shtahnt

51. Zulage
Tsoo-lahk-eh

52. Beförderung
Beh-fuhr-deh-roong

53. Betriebsschluss
Beh-treeps-shlooss

54. Lohn:
Lohn:

a. Stunden-
Shtoon-den-

b. Tages-
Tahk-es-

c. Wochen-
Voh-khen-

55. Wiederaufführung
Vee-der-owf-few-roong

56. Wiederholungsgebühr
Vee-der-hoh-loongs-geh-bewr

57. Pause
Pow-zeh

58. Zweites Team
Tsvye-tes Teh-ahm

59. Abfindung
Ahp-fin-doong

60. Stand-by

61. Start

62. Start Slip

63. Steward

64. Studio Zone

65. Technician

66. Temporary

67. Time:

a. -card

b. double

c golden (2½)

d. over-

e. straight

f. -and-one-half

g. triple

60. Ersatz- (mann, frau)
Ehr-zahts- (mahn, fr'ow)

61. Anfang
Ahn-fahng

62. Zeit Karte
Tsye't kahr-teh

63. Vertrauensperson im Betrieb
Fehr-tr'ow-enz-pehr-zohn ihm Beh-treep

64. Studiozone
Shtoo-d'yoh-tsoh-neh

65. Techniker
Tekh-nik-er

66. Vorübergehend
Foh-rew-behr-gay-ent

67. Zeit:
Tsye't:

a. Stechkarte
Shtekh-kahr-teh

b. zweifach
tsvye-fahkh

c. zweieinhalbfach
tsvye-eye'n-hahlp-fahkh

d. Überstunden
Ew-ber-shtoond-en

e. normal
nawr-mahl-

f. eineinhalbfach
eye'n-eh-eye'n-hahlp-fahkh

g. dreifach
dry-fahkh

68. Timekeeper

69. Time Worked:

a. days

b. hours

c. months

d. weeks

e. years

70. Travel Time

71. Union

72. Unemployed

73. Voucher

74. Wages

75. Wrap (quitting time)

68. Zeitnehmer
Tsite-neh-mer

69. Arbeitszeiten:
Ar-bites-tsite-en:

a. Tage
Tahk-eh

b. Stunden
Shtoon-den

c. Monate
Moh-naht-eh

d. Wochen
Vohkh-en

e. Jahre
Yah-reh

70. Reisezeit
Rye-zeh-tsite

71. Gewerkschaft
Geh-vehrk-shahft

72. Arbeitslos
Ar-bites-lohs

73. Gutschein
Goot-shine

74. Lohn
Lohn

75. Arbeitsschluss
Ar-bites-shlooss

01. Can you help me?

02. We wish to film/telecast in/by:

a. the mountains

b. the desert

c. the jungle

d. a large city

e. a small village

f. a river

g. the street

h. the road

i. the outskirts

j. the beach

k. a lake

l. offshore

m. a remote area

DRAY-AHRT

01. Können Sie mir helfen?
Kuh-nen Zee meer helf-en?

02. Wir möchten gerne in....filmen:
Veer muhkh-ten gehr-neh in....film-en:

a. den Bergen
denn Behr-gen

b. der Wüste
dehr Vew-steh

c. im Dschungel
ihm D'shoon-gel

d. einer grossen Stadt
eye'ner groh-sen Shtahdt

e. einem kleinem Dorf
eye-nem klye-nem Dawrf

f. einem Fluss
eye-nem Flooss

g. der Strasse
dehr Shtrah-seh

h. der Landstrasse
dehr Lahnt-shtrah-seh

i. ausserhalb der Stadt
owss-er-hahlp dehr Shtaht

j. am Strand
ahm Shtrahnt

k. am See
ahm Zay

l. im Meer
ihm Mayr

m. einer abgelegenen Gegend
eye-ner ahp-geh-lay-gen-en Gay-gent

02. We wish to film/telecast in/by (cont):

n. not too far from civilization

o. a busy thoroughfare

p. a quiet street

q. a residential area

r. an industrial area

s. a farm

03. We would like to scout it by:

a. airplane

b. boat

c. car

d. helicopter

e. horseback

04. Where can we rent one?

05. Is a map available?

02. Wir möchten gerne in....filmen (fort.):
Veer mukh-ten gehr-neh in..film-en(f):

n. nicht zu weit von der Zivilisation
nikht tsoo vite fahn dehr Tsih-vee-lih-zaht-s'yohn

o. einer verkehrsreichen Durchfahrtsstrasse
eye-ner fehr-keh-rye-khen Doorkh-fahrts-shtrah-seh

p. einer ruhigen Strasse
eye-ner roo-ih-gen Shtrah-seh

q. einer Wohngegend
eye-ner Vohn-geh-gehnt

r. einer Industriegegend
eye-ner In-doo-stree-geh-gehnt

s. einem Bauernhof
eye-nem B'ow-ern-hawf

03. Wir würden es uns gerne mit dem....ansehen:
Veer vewr-den ehs oons gehr-neh mit dem....ahn-zay-en:

a. Flugzeug
Flook-tsoyk

b. Schiff/Boot
Shiff/Boht

c. Auto
Ow-toh

d. Hubschrauber
Hoop-shr'ow-ber

e. zu Pferde
tsoo Pfehr-deh

04. Wo können wir einen/eines mieten?
Voh kuh-nen veer eye-nen/eye-nes meet-en?

05. Ist eine Landkarte zu haben?
Isst eye-neh Lahnt-kar-teh tsoo hah-ben?

06. How much will it cost?

a. per day

b. per hour

c. per week

07. Do we need permission to go there?

08. What must we do to get permission?

09. From whom?

10. For each person?

11. Will the permit cover everyone in our group?

12. How long will it take?

a. for someone to decide

b. to go there and return

13. We want to know ahead of time

06. Wievel wird das kosten?
Vee-feel veert dahss koh-sten?

a. pro Tag
proh Tahk

b. pro Stunde
proh Shtoon-deh

c. pro Woche
pro Voh-keh

07. Brauchen wir Erlaubnis um dahin zu gehen?
Br'owkh-en veer Ehr-l'owp-nis oom dah-hin tsoo gay-en?

08. Was müssen wir tun um
Vahss mewss-en veer toon oom

Erlaubnis zu bekommen?
Ehr-l'owp-nis tsoo beh-kohm-en?

09. Von wem?
Fahn vehm?

10. Für jede Person?
Fewr yay-deh Pehr-zohn?

11. Wird die Erlaubnis die
Veerd dee Ehr-l'owp-nis dee

ganze Gruppe miteinbeziehen?
gahnts-eh Groo-peh mit-eye'n-beh-tsee-en?

12. Wie lange wird es dauern:
Vee lahng-eh veerd ehs d'ow-ern

a. bis sich jemand entschliesst?
biss zikh yay-mahnt ent-shleest?

b. hin und zurück?
hin oont tsoo-rewk?

13. Wir möchten es gerne im Voraus wissen
Veer mukh-ten ehs gehr-neh ihm Fawr-owss viss-en

14. Must we present our documents when we arrive?

15. Who is the person that we contact?

16. Where do we find him/her?

17. Will we need...?

a. a guide

b. police escort

c. military escort

18. We wish to go to...

19. Is it far away?

20. Nearby?

21. Is there a bank there?

22. Is there a public telephone?

23. Are inoculations necessary?

14. Müssen wir unsere Dokumente
Mewss-en veer oon-zehr-eh Dah-koo-ment-eh

vorweisen bei unserer Ankunft?
fawr-vye-zen bye oon-zehr-er Ahn-koonft?

15. Zu wem müssen wir
Tsoo vehm mewss-en veer

Kontakt aufnehmen?
Kohn-tahkht owf-neh-men?

16. Wo können wir sie/ihn finden?
Voh kuh-nen veer zee/ihn fin-den?

17. Werden wir....benötigen?
Vehr-den veer....beh-nut-ih-gen?

a. einen Fremdenführer
eye-nen Frem-den-few-rer

b. eine Polizeieskorte
eye-neh Poh-lee-tsye-ehs-kohr-teh

c. eine Militäreskorte
eye-neh Mih-lih-ehr-ehs-kohr-teh

18. Wir möchten gerne nach...
Veer mukh-ten gehr-neh nahkh....

19. Ist es sehr weit weg?
Isst es Zehr vite vek?

20. In der Nähe?
In dehr Neh-heh?

21. Gibt es da eine Bank?
Gipt es dah eye-neh Bahnk?

22. Fin öffentliches Telefon?
Fin uhf-ent-likh-es Teh-leh-fohn?

23. Benötigen wir Schutzimpfungen?
Beh-nut-ih-gen veer Shoot-tsimp-foon-gen?

24. What facilities are available?

a. film laboratory

b. television station

c. equipment rental

d. caterer

25. Are there experienced personnel?

26. It is very expensive

27. Is everything included?

28. We do not have much time

29. We wish to:

a. take some photos

b. take a look at it

c. see if it will serve our purposes

d. talk to some people

24. Welche Einrichtungen gibt es hier:
Vehlkh-eh Eye'n-rikh-toon-gen gipt ehs heer:

a. Kopierwerk
Koh-peer-wehrk

b. Fernsehsender
Fehrn-zeh-zen-der

c. Geräteverleih
Geh-reht-eh-fehr-lye

d. gastronomische Lieferfirma
gahst-roh-noh-mish-eh Lee-fer-fir-mah

25. Gibt es erfahrenes Personal?
Gipt ehs ehr-fah-ren-es Pehr-zoh-nahl?

26. Es ist sehr teuer
Ehs isst zehr toy-er

27. Ist alles inbegriffen?
Isst ahl-les in-beh-grif-en?

28. Wir haben nicht viel Zeit
Veer hah-ben nikht feel Tsye't

29. Wir möchten gerne:
Veer mukh-ten gehr-neh:

a. ein paar Fotos machen
eye'n pahr Foh-tohs mahkh-en

b. es uns ansehen
ehs oons ahn-zay-en

c. sehen, ob es für unsere
zay-en, ohp ehs fewr oon-zehr-eh

Zwecke geeignet ist
Tsveh-kheh geh-eye'g-net isst

d. mit ein paar Leuten reden
mit eye'n pahr Loy-ten ray-den

29. We wish to (continued):

e. see a certain person

f. employ people

g. hire animals

h. rent equipment

30. We will need accomodations:

a. food

b. a good restaurant

c. lodgings

d. single

e. double

f. suite

g. with bath

h. air conditioning

i. quiet

29. Wir möchten gerne (fort.):
Veer mukh-ten gehr-neh (fawrt.):

e. eine bestimmte Person treffen
eye-neh beh-shtim-teh Pehr-zohn treh-fen

f. Leute anstellen
Loy-teh ahn-shtellen

g. Tiere mieten
Tee-reh mee-ten

h. Geräte mieten
Geh-reht-eh mee-ten

30. Wir brauchen Quartier:
Veer br'owkh-en Kvahr-teer:

a. Essen/Verpflegung
Ess-en/Fehr-pfleh-goon

b. ein gutes Restaurant
eye'n goo-tehs Reh-staw-rahnt

c. Unterkunft
Oon-ter-koonft

d. Einzelzimmer
Eye'n-tsel-tsim-mer

e. Doppelzimmer
Dop-pel-tsim-mer

f. Suite
Sweet

g. mit Bad
mit Baht

h. Klimaanlage
Klim-ah-ahn-lah-geh

i. ruhig
roo-ik

30. We will need accomodations (cont):

j. tent

k. camping gear

l. beer

m. whiskey

31. If we dislike something

we are annoyed

32. You are very kind

33. We will be in that

location for:

a. days

b. weeks

c. months

d. a short time

e. a long time

30. Wir brauchen Quartier (fort.):
Veer br'owkh-en Kvahr-teer (fawrt.):

j. Zelt
Tsellt

k. Lagerausstattung
Lah-ger-owss-shtaht-toong

l. Bier
Beer

m. Whisky
Wisk-ee

31. Wenn uns etwas nicht gefällt,
Venn oons eht-vahs nikht geh-fellt,

sind wir verärgert
zint veer fehr-ehr-gehrt

32. Sie sind sehr freundlich
Zee zint zehr froynd-likh

33. Wir werden an diesem
Veer vehr-den ahn dee-zem

Drehort für....sein:
Dray-ahrt fewr.....zine:

a. Tage
Tah-keh

b. Wochen
Vohkh-en

c. Monate
Moh-nah-teh

d. eine kurze Zeit
eye-neh koort-tseh Tsite

e. eine lange Zeit
eye-neh lahn-geh Tsite

34. We will transport the crew by:

a. bus

b. plane

c. train

d. car

e. wagon

f. ship

g. boat

35. Wear:

a. light clothing

b. winter clothing

c. boots

d. raingear

e. sun hat

f. gloves

34. Wir werden das Team mit dem....befördern:
Veer vehr-den dahss Tay-ahm mit dem.... beh-fuhr-dehrn:

a. Bus
Booss

b. Flugzeug
Flook-tsoyk

c. Zug
Tsook

d. Auto
Ow-toh

e. Wagen
Vah-gen

f. Schiff
Shiff

g. Boot
Boht

35. Kleidung:
Klye-doong:

a. Sommerkleidung
Zahm-er-klye-doong

b. Winterkleidung
Vin-ter-klye-doong

c. Stiefel
Shteef-el

d. Regenmantel
Ray-gen-mahn-tel

e. Sonnenhut
Zahn-en-hoot

f. Handschuhe
Hahnt-shoo-heh

36. Beware of:

a. snakes

b. reptiles

c. insects

d. wild animals

37. Take insect repellant

38. We will arrive at our destination:

a. on time

b. late

c. early

39. Where can I cash traveler's checks?

40. Where can I exchange my country's currency for yours?

36. Achtung vor:
Ahkh-toong fohr:

a. Schlangem
Shlahng-em

b. Reptilien
Rep-til-een

c. Insekten
In-zek-ten

d. wilden Tieren
vil-den Teer-en

37. Insektenspray mitnehmen
In-zek-ten-shpray mit-neh-men

38. Wir werden....an unserem Ziel ankommen:
Veer vehr-den....ahn oon-zehr-em Tseel ahn-kohm-en:

a. zur erwarteten Zeit
tsoor ehr-vahr-teh-ten Tsite

b. spät
shpayt

c. früher
frew-er

39. Wo kann ich
Voh kahn ikh

Reisechecks einlösen?
Rye-zeh-sheks eye'n-luh-zen?

40. Wo kann ich
Voh kahn ikh

Geld wechseln?
Gelt vekh-zehln?

41. What is the rate of exchange today?

42. At least one room on the ground floor for the equipment

43. We have arrived

44. This is the place

45. We must leave

46. This will not do

47. We will go elsewhere

48. How much will this cost?

49. Too expensive

50. Inexpensive

51. There is an extra charge for that

52. Is that clear?

41. Was ist der
Vahss isst dehr

heutige Wechselkurs?
hoy-tik-eh Vehkh-zel-koorz?

42. Zumindest einen Raum im Erdgeshoss
Tsoo-min-dehst eye-nen R'owm ihm Ehrt-geh-shawss

für die Geräte
fewr dee Geh-reht-eh

43. Wir sind angekommen
Veer zint ahn-geh-kohm-men

44. Das ist der Platz
Dahss isst dehr Plahts

45. Wir müssen weg
Veer mewss-en vek

46. Das genügt nicht
Dahss geh-newkt nikht

47. Wir werden woanders hingehen
Veer vehr-den voh-ahn-ders hin-gay-en

48. Wieviel wird das kosten?
Vee-feel veerd dahss koh-sten?

49. Zu teuer
Tsoo toy-er

50. Billig/Preiswert
Bill-ik/Prize-vert

51. Da ist ein extra Aufschlag dafür
Dah isst eye'n eks-trah Owf-shlahk dah-fewr

52. Ist das klar?
Isst dahss klahr?

53. That is my final offer

54. We do not spend money foolishly

55. This is a business venture

56. We are not tourists, we are here to work

57. What did you say?

58. I must have your answer now

59. I haven't much time

60. Think about it

61. Exactly

62. Agreed

63. Location work is difficult

64. It requires attention to details

53. Das ist mein endgültiges Angebot!
Dahss isst mine ent-gewl-tih-gehs Ahn-geh-boht!

54. Wir schmeissen nicht umsonst Geld raus!
Veer shmye-sen nikht oom-zohnst Gehlt r'owss!

55. Das ist eine geshäftliche Angelegenheit
Dahss isst eye-neh geh-sheft-likh-eh Ahn-geh-lay-gen-hite

56. Wir sind keine Touristen, wir sind hier um zu arbeiten
Veer zint kye-neh Too-rist-en, veer zint heer oom tsoo ar-bye-ten

57. Was haben Sie gesagt?
Vahss hah-ben Zee geh-zahkt?

58. Ich muss Ihre Antwort jetzt haben
Ikh mooss Ih-reh Ahnt-vohrt yetst hah-ben

59. Ich habe nicht viel Zeit
Ikh hah-beh nikht feel Tsite

60. Überlegen Sie sich es noch einmal
Ew-ber-lay-gen Zee zikh ehs nokh eye'n-mahl

61. Genau
Geh-n'ow

62. Einverstanden
Eye'n-fehr-shtahn-den

63. Die Arbeit an Drehort ist schwierig
Dee Ar-bite ahn Dray-ahrt isst Shveer-ik

64. Mann muss jedem Detail Aufmerksamkeit schenken
Mahn mooss yay-dem Deh-tile Owf-mehrk-zahm-kite shen-ken

01. Name of consignor (shipper)

02. Name of consignee (receiver)

03. Last name

04. First name

05. Address

06. Via:

a. air

b. ship

c. train

d. truck

07. Is the address on each case?

08. What carrier?

09. I shall carry this myself

10. Here is:

a. my passport

01. Name des Senders
Nah-meh dess Zen-ders

02. Name des Empfängers
Nah-meh dess Emp-feng-ers

03. Nachname
Nahkh-nah-meh

04. Vorname
Fohr-nah-meh

05. Adresse
Ah-dress-eh

06. Über:
Ew-ber:

a. Luftpost
Looft-pohst

b. Schiffpost
Shiff-pohst

c. Bahnversand
Bahn-fehr-zahnt

d. Spedition
Shpay-dit-s'yohn

07. Ist die Adresse auf jedem Koffer?
Isst dee Ah-dress-ef owf yay-dem Kaw-fer?

08. Welche Fluglinie?
Velkh-eh Flook-lin-ee?

09. Ich werde das selber tragen
Ikh vehr-deh dahss zel-ber trah-gen

10. Hier ist mein:
Heer isst mine:

a. Reisepass
Rye-zeh-pahss

10. Here is (continued):

 b. my identification

 c. my visa

 d. my work permit

 e. my airbill

 f. my waybill

 g. my equipment list

11. Here are the baggage checks

12. I have _____ pieces

of equipment and _____

pieces of personal luggage

13. That is not mine

14. That one is mine

15. One item is missing

16. Check with lost and found

10. Hier ist mein (fort.):
    Heer isst mine (fawrt.):

    b. Ausweiss
       Owss-vise

    c. Visum
       Vih-zoom

    d. Arbeitserlaubnis
       Ar-bites-er-l'owp-nis

    e. Luftfrachtrechnung
       Looft-rahkht-rekh-noong

    f. Frachtrechnung
       Frahkht-rekh-noong

    g. Ausstattungsliste
       Owss-shtaht-toongs-lis-teh

11. Hier sind die Gepäcksscheine
    Heer zint die Geh-pehks-shine-eh

12. Ich habe....Teile berufliches
    Ikh hah-beh....Tye-leh beh-roof-likh-es

    Gepäck und....
    Geh-pehk oont....

    Teile persönliches Gepäck
    Tye-leh pehr-zuhn-likh-es Geh-pehk

13. Das gehört nicht mir
    Dahss geh-huhrt nikht meer

14. Das gehört mir
    Dahss geh-huhrt meer

15. Etwas fehlt
    Et-vahss fehlt

16. Erkundigen Sie sich in Fundbüro
    Ehr-koont-ih-gen Zee Zikh ihn Foont-bew-roh

17. Must we open each case?

18. I have nothing to declare

19. Regulations are regulations

20. Can we hasten this someway?

21. It is against regulations

22. This is all I have to declare

23. This cannot be opened for inspection

24. Why not?

25. It will be ruined if exposed to light

26. But it must be inspected

27. I cannot permit it

28. Then it cannot go through

29. Who is in charge here?

17. Müssen wir jeden Koffer öffnen?
Mewss-en veer yay-den Kaw-fer uhf-nen?

18. Ich habe nichts zu verzollen
Ikh hah-beh nikht tsoo fehr-tsohl-len

19. Vorschriften sind Vorschriften!
Fohr-shrif-ten zint Fohr-shrif-ten!

20. Können wir das irgendwie beschleunigen?
Kuh-nen veer dahss ihr-gent-vee beh-shloy-nih-gen?

21. Es ist gegen die Vorschriften
Ess isst gay-gen dee Fohr-shrift-en

22. Das ist alles was ich zu verzollen habe
Dahss isst ahl-les vahss ikh hah-ben tsoo fehr-tsoh-len hah-ben

23. Das kann nicht geöffnet
Dahss kahn nikht geh-uff-net

werden
vehr-den

24. Warum nicht?
Vah-room nikht?

25. Lichtenfall ruinert
Likht-en-fahl roo-in-ehrt

den Inhalt
dehn In-hahlt

26. Aber es muss kontrolliert werden
Ah-ber ehs mooss Kohn-trohl-eert vehr-den

27. Ich kann es nicht erlauben
Ikh kahn es nikht ehr-l'owp-en

28. Dann kann es nicht durch den Zoll
Dahn kahn es nikht doorkh den Tsohl

29. Wer trägt hier die Verantwortung?
Vehr trekt heer dee Fehr-ahnt-vohr-toong?

30. What is his name?

31. I would like to see him

32. What is your name?

33. How long will it take?

34. We registered the equipment

before we left

35. The rawstock also

36. We will purchase rawstock

here and send it home

after it has been exposed

37. We will pay duty on it

38. The name of the custom

broker is ____

39. I have a registry receipt

for the equipment and rawstock

30. Wie heisst er?
Vee hye-st ehr?

31. Ich wünsche ihn zu sprechen
Ikh vuhn-sheh ihn tsoo shprekh-en

32. Wie heissen Sie?
Vee hye-sehn Zee?

33. Wie lange wird es dauern?
Vee lahn-geh veerd ehs d'ow-ern?

34. Wir hadieses Ausrüstung vor unserer
Veer hah-dee-zes Owss-rewst-oong fawr oon-zehr-er
Abreise eintragen lassen
Ah-brye-zeh eye'n-trah-gen lahss-en

35. Auch den Rohfilm
Ow'kh dehn Roh-film

36. Wir werden Rohfilm hier
Veer vehr-den Roh-film heer
kaufen und nach seiner
k'ow-fehn oont nahkh zye'n-er
Belichtung nach Hause senden
Beh-likh-toong nahkh How-zeh zen-den

37. Wir werden Zollgebühren dafur bezahlen
Veer vehr-den Tsohl-geh-bew-ren dah-foor beh-tsahl-en

38. Der Name des
Dehr Nah-meh dess
Zoll-Maklers ist....
Tsohl-mahk-lers isst...

39. Ich habe einen Registrierbeleg für
Ikh hah-beh eye-nen Reh-gih-streer-beh-leg fewr
die Ausrüstung und den Rohfilm
dee Owss-rewst-oong oont dehn Roh-film

40. Here is the manifest

41. Each item is listed with:

a. a serial number and weight

b. the country where it was manufactured

42. When we ship,

we always notify

our customs broker

43. We also send the

airbill/waybill number

and announce when the

shipment is due to arrive

44. We also attach all

the numbers of the

airbill/waybill

to each case

40. Hier ist die Geräteliste
Heer isst dee Geh-reht-eh-lihst-eh

41. Neben jedem Gegenstand ist aufgeschrieban:
Nay-ben yay-dem Geh-gehn-shtahnt isst owf-geh-shree-bahn:

a. die Seriennummer unt Gewicht
dee Zeh-reen-noo-mer oont Geh-vikht

b. das Herstellungsland
dahss Hehr-shtell-oonks-lahnt

42. Wenn wir etwas versenden
Venn veer eht-vahss fehr-zen-den

verständigen wir unseren
fehr-shten-dik-en veer oon-zehr-en

Zollabfertigungsmakler
Tsohl-lahp-fehr-tik-goongs-mahk-ler

43. Wir senden auch die Luftfracht/
Veer zen-den ow'kh dee Looft-frahkht/

Frachtnummer und benachrichtigen den
Frahkht-noo-mer oont beh-nakh-rikh-tih-gen dehn

Empfänger über den voraussichtlichen
Emp-fen-ger ew-ber dehn fawr-owss-zikht-likh-en

Ankunftstermin der Sendung
Ahn-koonft-shtehr-mihn dehr Zen-doong

44. Wir kleben auch
Veer klay-ben owkh

an alle Kisten
ahn ahl-eh Kih-sten

die Luftfrachtnummern/
dee Looft-frakht-noom-ern/

Frachtnummern
Frakht-noo-mern

45. The customs broker charges

a service fee

for each shipment

46. Don't forget to add

freight fee charged

by the carrier

47. In some countries,

one has to pay additional

tax for

exposed film upon

leaving

48. Often there is a delivery

charge for film between

point of entry

and the laboratory

45. Der Zollmakler verlangt
Dehr Tsohl-mahk-ler fehr-lahnkt

für jede Sendung
fewr yay-deh Zen-doong

eine Abfertigungsgebühr
eye-neh Ahp-fewr-tik-oongs-geh-bewr

46. Vergessen Sie nicht
Fehr-gehss-en Zee nikht

die Transportkosten des
dee Trahnz-pawrt-koh-sten dehss

Zustellers dazuzurechnen
Tsoo-shtell-ers dah-tsoo-tsoo-rekh-nen

47. In manchen Ländern
In mahn-khen Len-dern

wird eine separate
veert eye-neh zep-ah-rah-teh

Gebühr
Geh-bewr

für belichteten Film
fewr beh-likh-teh-ten Film

verlangt
fehr-lahnkt

48. Oft wird auch eine Zustellungsgebühr
Ohft veert owkh eye-neh Tsoo-shtell-oongs-geh-bewr

für die Zustellung des Films
fewr dee Tsoo-shtell-oong dehss Films

vom Hafen/Flughafen
fahm Hah-fen/Flook-hah-fen

zum Kopierwerk verlangt
tsoom Koh-peer-vehrk fehr-lahnkt

49. Is this equipment

being imported?

50. Not at all

51. It is being brought in for

use on a production

52. Then, we will take it back

53. If that is not stated

you will have to pay

an import tax

54. How can we get this through

customs quickly?

55. Be sure to get your papers

stamped: Passed

56. Never try to smuggle anything

in or out

49. Werden diese Geräte
Vehr-den dee-zeh Geh-reht-eh

importiert?
im-pawr-teert?

50. Naturlich nickht
Nah-toor-likh nikht

51. Diese Geräte werden für die
Dee-zeh Geh-reht-eh vehr-den fewr dee

Dreharbeiten gebraucht
Dray-ar-bite-en geh-br'owkht

52. Dann werden wir sie wieder ausführen
Dahn vehr-den veer zee vee-der owss-fewr-en

53. Wenn das nicht klar ausgedrückt wird
Venn dahss nikht klahr owss-geh-drewkt veert

müssen Sie eine
mewss-en Zee eye-neh

Importsteuer Zahlen
Im-pawrt-shtoy-er Tsah-len

54 Wie können wir schnell durch die
Vee kuhn-en veer shnell doorkh dee

Zollabfertigung kommen?
Tsohl-ahp-fehr-tik-oong kohm-en?

55. Sie sollten immer überprüfen, ob Sie
Zee zohl-ten ihm-mer ew-ber-prew-fen, ohp Zee

den Kontrollstempel au allen Papieren haben
dehn Kohn-trohl-shtem-pel ow ahl-en Pah-peer-en hah-ben

56. Schmuggeln Sie nichts
Shmoog-geln Zee nikhts

Useful Terms:

57. Enter

58. Exit

59. Customs Inspection

60. Customs Broker

61. Carrier

62. Freight Pickup and Receiving

63. Passport Office

64. Immigration

Nützliche Begriffe:
Newt-slikh-eh Beh-grif-eh:

57. Eingang
Eye'n-gahng

58. Ausgang
Owss-gahng

59. Zollkontrolle
Tsohl-kohn-troh-leh

60. Zollmakler
Tsohl-mahk-ler

61. Spediteur
Shped-ih-tewr

62. Frachtur Ausgabe und Annahme
Frahkh-toor Owss-gah-beh oont Ahn-nahm-eh

63. Passkontrolle
Pahss-kohn-troh-leh

64. Ausländerbehörde
Owss-lehnt-er-beh-huhr-deh

Time:

01. Year

02. Month

a. January

b. February

c. March

d. April

e. May

f. June

g. July

h. August

i. September

j. October

k. November

l. December

Zeit:
Tsite:

01. Jahr
Yahr

02. Monat:
Moh-naht

a. Januar
Yahn-oo-ahr

b. Februar
Fay-broo-ahr

c. März
Mehrts

d. April
Ah-pril

e. Mai
Mye

f. Juni
Yoo-nee

g. Juli
Yoo-lee

h. August
Ow-goost

i. September
Zep-tem-ber

j. Oktober
Ahk-toh-ber

k. November
Nah-vem-ber

l. Dezember
Dayt-sem-ber

Time (continued):

03. Week:

a. Monday

b. Tuesday

c. Wednesday

d. Thursday

e. Friday

f. Saturday/Sunday

04. Day

05. Hour

06. Minute

07. Second

08. Dawn

09. Morning

10. Noon

Zeit (fort.):
Tsite (fawrt.):

03. Woche:
Vohkh-eh:

a. Montag
Mohn-tahk

b. Dienstag
Deens-tahk

c. Mittwoch
Mitt-vohkh

d. Donnerstag
Dahn-ers-tahk

e. Freitag
Fry-tahk

f. Samstag/Sonntag
Zahms-tahk/Zahn-tahk

04. Tag
Tahk

05. Stunde
Shtoon-deh

06. Minute
Mih-noot-eh

07. Sekunde
Zeh-koond-eh

08. Morgen
Mawr-gen

09. Mittag
Mit-tahk

10. Nacht
Nahkht

Time (continued):

11. Afternoon

12. Dusk

13. Night

14. Midnight

15. A.M.

16. P.M.

17. Early

18. Late

19. On Time

20. Today

21. Tomorrow

22. Yesterday

23. Day after tomorrow

24. Day before yesterday

Zeit (fort.):
Tsite (fawrt.):

11. Abend
Ah-bent

12. Morgendämmerung
Mawr-gen-dem-er-oong

13. Abenddämmerung
Ah-bent-dem-er-oong

14. Mitternacht
Mit-ter-nahkht

15. Vor Mittag
Fawr Mit-tahk

16. Nach Mittag
Nahkh Mit-tahk

17. Früh
Frew

18. Spät
Shpayt

19. Pünktlich
Pewnkt-likh

20. Heute
Hoy-teh

21. Morgen
Mawr-gen

22. Gestern
Geh-shtehrn

23. Übermorgen
Ew-ber-mawr-gen

24. Vorgestern
Fawr-geh-shtehrn

Numbers:

25. One

26. Two

27. Three

28. Four

29. Five

30. Six

31. Seven

32. Eight

33. Nine

34. Ten

35. Eleven

36. Twelve

37. Thirteen

38. Fourteen

Zahlen:
Tsah-len

25. Eins
Eye'ns

26. Zwei
Tsvye

27. Drei
Dry

28. Vier
Feer

29. Fünf
Fewnf

30. Sechs
Zekhs

31. Sieben
Zee-ben

32. Acht
Ahkht

33. Neun
Noyn

34. Zehn
Tsehn

35. Elf
Ehlf

36. Zwölf
Tsvuhlf

37. Dreizehn
Dry-tsehn

38. Vierzehn
Feer-tsehn

Numbers (continued):

39. Fifteen

40. Twenty

41. Thirty

42. Forty

43. Fifty

44. Sixty

45. Seventy

46. Eighty

47. Ninety

48. Hundred

49. Thousand

50. Million

51. Billion

52. Trillion

Zahlen (fort.):
Tsah-len (fawrt.):

39. Fünfzehn
Fewnf-tsehn

40. Zwanzig
Tsvahn-tsik

41. Dreissig
Drys-sik

42. Vierzig
Feer-tsik

43. Fünfzig
Fewnf-tsik

44. Sechzig
Zekh-tsik

45. Siebzig
Zeeb-tsik

46. Achtzig
Ahkt-sik

47. Neunzig
Noyn-tsik

48. Hundert
Hoon-dehrt

49. Tausend
T'ow-zehnt

50. Million
Mihl-ih-ohn

51. Billion
Bihl-ih-ohn

52. Trillion
Trihl-ih-ohn

Math:

53. Add

54. Subtract

55. Divide

56. Multiply

57. Circle

58. Square

59. Rectangle

60. Circumference

61. Diameter

62. Segment

63. Half

64. Quarter

65. Three-quarters

Mathematik:
Mah-teh-mah-teek:

53. Addieren/Zusammenzählen
Ah-deer-en/Tsoo-zahm-en-tseh-len

54. Subtrahieren/Abziehen
Zoop-trah-heer-en/Ahp-tsee-en

55. Dividieren/Teilen
Dih-vih-deer-en/Tye-len

56. Multiplizieren/Malnehmen
Mool-tee-plih-tseer-en/Mahl-neh-men

57. Kreis
Kry-ss

58. Quadrat
Kvah-draht

59. Rechteck
Rekh-tek

60. Umfang
Oom-fahng

61. Diameter
Dih-ah-may-ter

62. Segment
Zeg-ment

63. Hälfte
Helf-teh

64. Viertel
Feer-tel

65. Dreiviertel
Dry-feer-tel

Weather:

66. Clear

67. Cloudy

68. Cold

69. Fog

70. Hail

71. Hot

72. Humid

73. Overcast

74. Rain

75. Sleet

76. Snow

77. Sunny

78. Variable

79. Windy

Wetter:
Vett-er:

66. Klar
Klahr

67. Wolkig
Vohl-kik

68. Kalt
Kahlt

69. Nebel
Nay-bel

70. Hagel
Hah-gel

71. Heiss
Hye-ss

72. Feucht
Foykht

73. Bewölkt
Beh-vuhlkt

74. Regen
Ray-gen

75. Eisregen
Eye's-ray-gen

76. Schnee
Shnay

77. Sonnig
Zahn-ik

78. Veränderlich
Fehr-ehn-dehr-likh

79. Windig
Vin-dik

ADDITIONAL TERMS

SECTION	PAGE	TERM

ADDITIONAL TERMS

SECTION	PAGE	TERM

ADDITIONAL TERMS

SECTION	PAGE	TERM

ADDITIONAL TERMS

SECTION	PAGE	TERM

NEED MORE BOOKS?
order from

YOUR BOOKSELLER, or
DOUBLE C Publishing Company
120 East Verdugo Avenue
Burbank, California 91502

Please Reserve:

Set of FIVE...OR individual volume of

French......German......Italian......

Spanish....Japanese......

POSTAGE & HANDLING	SET	EACH
USA (AIRMAIL)	$ 7.50	$4.00
USA (SURFACE)	$ 2.50	$1.00
OVERSEAS (AIRMAIL)	$25.00	$6.00
OVERSEAS (SURFACE)	$ 4.00	$1.50

In California ADD 6½% Sales Tax

INDIVIDUAL
VOLUMES
AVAILABLE
at
$17.95* ea.

*Exclusive of
Postage & Handling

Name(Print)..............................
Address..............................
City..............................
State.......................Zip.......

I enclose check/International Money
order for $.......................

NEED MORE BOOKS?
order from

YOUR BOOKSELLER, or
DOUBLE C Publishing Company
120 East Verdugo Avenue
Burbank, California 91502

Please Reserve:

Set of FIVE...OR individual volume of

French......German......Italian......

Spanish.....Japanese......

POSTAGE & HANDLING	SET	EACH
USA (AIRMAIL)	$ 7.50	$4.00
USA (SURFACE)	$ 2.50	$1.00
OVERSEAS (AIRMAIL)	$25.00	$6.00
OVERSEAS (SURFACE)	$ 4.00	$1.50

In California ADD 6½% Sales Tax

INDIVIDUAL VOLUMES AVAILABLE at $17.95* ea.

*Exclusive of Postage & Handling

Name(Print)..............................
Address..................................
City.....................................
State........................Zip.......

I enclose check/International Money order for $......................